Pure Water

The Beauty and Mystery

Of Baptism

Copyright © 2012 Chase McMaster

Published by Pilgrim Voyage Press 2013, www.pilgrimvoyage.com

All rights reserved. No part of this publication may be reproduced or transmitted in any form or by any means, electronic or mechanical, including photocopy, recording, or any information storage and retrieval system for the purpose of sales, marketing, or distribution, without written consent of the publisher or author.

Cover design by Pilgrim Voyage Press

All Scripture taken from the New King James Version; italics belong to the author

Printed in the United States of America

ISBN 978-0-9891166-2-6

To Andy F, Nate E, & Bryan J

I have greatly enjoyed your fellowship and our profitable
discussions
Peace to you and your families

TABLE OF CONTENTS

Preface/ 7

Part One – What is Baptism?

1. A Ritual/ 13
2. A Sacrament/ 22
3. The Commonality of Confessions/ 29
4. The Dissenting View/ 37
5. The Christian/ 45
6. Law or Gospel?/ 51
7. Election/ 58

Part Two – What does Baptism do?

8. Making Christians/ 65
9. Signs and Seals/ 69
10. Union with Christ/ 75
11. Remission of Sins/ 82
12. Assurance/ 87
13. Washing of Regeneration/ 95
14. Baptism and the Wardrobe/ 103
15. The Saving Power of Baptism/ 105

Part Three – Children in the Church

16. A House for My Name/ 110
17. You and Your Children/ 115

18. Meditations on Children and Slaves/ 124
19. The Case for Infant Baptism/ 138
20. Children of the New Covenant/ 145
21. Pilgrim's Progress Theology/ 153
22. A Multi-Generational Vision/ 163
23. Concluding Practical Inquiries/ 168
    Endnotes/ 173

"The wonderful privilege and the awful danger that comes with the place our children have in the church lie in close proximity. They are children of the kingdom – what could be more glorious! But they could be cast out into outer darkness – what could be more awful! The only way to avoid the latter is to fully grasp the former..."

~ Andrew Murray

"It's an extraordinary coincidence, isn't it? Baptized at two years old, and then beginning to go back to what you can't even remember...It's like an infection."

"It's what you say an odd coincidence."

~ From the End of the Affair

By Graham Greene

PREFACE

"I do not pray for these alone, but also for those who will believe in Me through their word; that they all may be one, as You, Father, are in Me, and I in You; that they also may be one in Us, that the world may believe that You sent Me. And the glory which You gave Me I have given them, that they may be one just as We are one: I in them, and You in Me; that they may be made perfect in one, and that the world may know that You have sent Me, and have loved them as You have loved Me." (John 17.20-23)

It should be no secret that a large portion of the glory of the Godhead exists in its unity. This is the unity which Christ acknowledges, and this is the unity for which he prayed. He prayed that the very union which exists between the eternal Father and the eternal Son would be replicated in human relationships – relationships between those people whom Christ came to redeem. Christ prayed that the unity among his people would be as strong as the unity between himself and his Father.

This unity, among other things, is a matter of divine parenting. When the Father takes his children out of the house, he does not want them quarreling in public. He does not want them looking disheveled. Rather, he wants order. He wants a united front. This unity is for the glory of the Godhead. This unity is a matter of how the church dresses up. In other words, the manner in which the church is presented before the watching world is of supreme importance to God. This united front is so important, in fact, that complete unity among his people is a testimony of Christ's lordship over his people – and not only so, but his lordship over the whole world. This is evidenced by his praying "…so that the world may know that You have sent Me."

That Christ wants unity within the church is nowhere in dispute. But what kind of unity does he desire? In what areas is this unity to be found? And to what extent?

It is the intent of this book to show that at the very least Christ desires unity in the practice of who we allow in the church. Above this end, there is a great surplus of things to be united about, but those are not the aim here. The present aim is to address the grievous disunity in the church which is manifested in the widespread practice of excluding certain individuals from church membership whom God, in his word, has clearly included. Those individuals are children.

God has a family. Therefore, he has children. He has rightful heirs. Unity will be an impossible task if we continue to disagree about who these children are. Is this not a foundational matter? The matter of who is to be rightfully admitted into the fellowship of the church must be settled if we are ever to begin moving toward unity in other matters. How can a family be in harmony when it perpetually disagrees upon who belongs in the family? This is the issue which is facing us today just as it has been facing us for five hundred years and even more. In fact, this issue plagued the church from the very beginning in regard to the inclusion of Gentiles. But for the sake of Christ's prayer as expressed in John 17, it is imperative that the church begin moving toward greater agreement in this area, and it will never be acceptable to simply overlook it.

The issue is no longer about Gentiles, but about baptism and what to do with all these Christian children, if indeed they can be called Christian children. They are children who are born into a household of faith. They are children who enter into a Christian home. They are children of believing parents. Are they members of the church or not? Should they be baptized or not? Should they have fellowship or not? Do they belong to Christ or not? Are they Christians or not?

Why do we tend to look past this important issue? Why have so many of us given up the struggle for unity in this area? Why is the evangelical church apparently split down the middle in this matter? How have we grown so content with this glaring schism?

If it is unity that Christ desires, we should not grow tired of working towards it. But when it comes to baptizing children, the two sides will barely budge. What ends up happening is that we begin to tolerate the other position. Tolerance is not unity.

Do we really think that if this matter is not settled that we will ever gain unity in the other matters of the gospel? Is this question of what to do with our children not a question of the gospel itself? When Christ says, "On this rock I will build My church, and the gates of Hades shall not prevail against it," (Matt. 16,18) is this not the gospel message? In this case, is it not essential that we understand what this church is that he is building? If not – if somehow we miss the mark – if we fail to grasp the full meaning of who the church is, then we miss an essential ingredient in the gospel recipe. Who does God say his children are? What is the extent of the gospel call? Is the gospel really powerful enough to lay claim upon all those it seems to want to lay claim over? Or should we wait upon our children to make their own decisions once they are old enough to discern for themselves? Do we not tell them who they are? Do we even know who our children are?

This book will attempt to show that children of Christian households belong to Christ and consequently should be considered members of his church with the right to water baptism. This is important because it is a matter of what the kingdom looks like. It is a matter of dressing up properly. It is a matter of basic unity because we already know, as someone important once said, that a kingdom divided against itself will not stand. (Mark 3,24)

Apologia

This book is an argument in favor of the practice of infant baptism, or what is commonly called 'paedobaptism' in theological discourse. With that being said, it is hopefully also much more than that. It is meant as a plea for unity in church ordinances and church fellowship. I will be referring to a certain faction of the church as dissenters. The reason is that at one point in history, or maybe in some respects over the course of time, those in this group have pulled away, or dissented, from the commonly held position on baptism. They have come to be known as Baptists, or even earlier, Anabaptists. I will call them Baptists in this book. In a broad sense, I use the term as a label for all those who believe that the only worthy recipients of baptism are those who actually profess repentance towards God, faith in, and obedience to, our Lord Jesus Christ; in other words, those who possess the cognitive ability to repent and believe and who have articulated the faith which they possess. However, I understand that all Baptists do not believe exactly the same in all areas, though they do share in common the belief that infants should not be baptized. It might be that some reading this book do not think of themselves as Baptists but do believe in the Baptist conception of church ordinances. It is the latter situation to which I apply the term.

Furthermore, I will use the term 'sacramentalist' to refer to those who hold a contrary belief to the Baptists, specifically the belief that infants in believing households are already covenant members and should therefore be baptized, despite their inability to articulate faith. I use this term 'sacramentalist' in the plainest sense possible, meaning those who believe in the use of sacraments; in other words, those who believe that the ordinances of God are actual means that God uses to bring about salvation. Though the term may carry other connotations not meant in this book, I can think of no better word to describe the difference between the two sides depicted here.

This book is not merely intended to be an endorsement of paedobaptism (the practice of including infants in baptism) over credobaptism (the practice of baptizing professing Christians only). Rather it is meant to be an endorsement of a sacramental conception of salvation over a baptistic conception. I hope the following pages will make the distinction clearer and show how the existence of that distinction is sadly nothing more than discord in the matter of the gospel.

PART ONE

WHAT IS BAPTISM?

1
A RITUAL

If baptism is anything, it is at the very least a ceremonial cleansing. The fact that it is much more should be plain enough, but baptism is certainly nothing less. It is at its very core a religious ritual.

This is one of the great problems with us moderns. We don't value ritual – at least not as we associate it with religion. After all, religious ritual belongs to pagans, ancients, and charlatans. We have become adept at removing just about all religion from ritual, and we call it tradition. In fact, we are quite content with having a picnic every 4th of July or watching a movie and eating popcorn every Friday night. We might have a habit of putting our pants on before our socks or singing 'Happy Birthday' before cutting the cake. Whatever it is, whether we call it habit or tradition, it testifies to the human need for ritual. God made us that way. Yet when it comes to religion, rituals often will not do. We don't want to eat the Lord's Supper too often in fear that it might become mundane. We don't want our ministers wearing robes because we don't want to appear too formal. We don't want to kneel when we pray because it looks weird. We want to avoid anything which resembles conformity, anything that appears too ritualistic. It is alright to raise our hands and shout provided it is a spontaneous act prompted by God himself, provided it is not a preplanned fabrication of spirituality. No, we want to avoid doing the same things over and over again in the same way. Yet God forbid we forget to set the donuts and coffee out on the table after church each week.

When we practice rituals without religion, we are left with bare tradition. We are creating habits for no other reason than custom and personal preference. It is not always wrong, but it is like removing the score from a baseball game. In that case, the players would be doing nothing more than going through the motions and maybe getting a little exercise. Certainly, they would not be competing. Tradition, for its own sake, without reason, is often meaningless. But when we do the opposite, when we practice a form of religion without rituals and call it 'spirituality' or even 'Christianity', we are left with something undefinable. It is like removing the shapes from a drawing. Without shapes, what kind of drawing do we have left?

Religion and ritual go together. Even though quite often every attempt has been made to divorce the religion from the ritual, it cannot be done because ritual is by its very nature religious. So in our attempts to strip away the religion from the ritual, calling it tradition, or to pry the ritual out of the religion calling it 'spirituality', we have in essence replaced one form of religion with another. We still do things, but we just do different things. We dedicate babies instead of pouring water on them. With adults, we call them forward and pray with them instead of getting them all wet. We have substituted one belief system for another. We will always have some sort of ritual, but we can have a tendency to remove the religion along with its meaning. For instance, we can take away the Christ, but keep the Christmas. We cannot shake our human need for ritual.

Jesus, let us not forget, was born into the heart of ritual. The good doctor, Luke, takes great care to make sure we know this, recording for us the various rituals of which Jesus partook before he was even able to understand what was happening to him. And yes, that is significant, the fact that he was too young to understand. He was circumcised upon the eighth day after his birth (Luke 2.21, Gen. 17.12), a rather important ritual without which Jesus would not even be counted among the people of God. In fact, he would have been cut off (Gen. 17.14), no doubt a testimony to God's ironic yet no less grotesque sense of humor. Furthermore, he was given his name during this ceremony, a name which meant something very appropriate and which was bestowed upon him by God himself. Yes, unlike us irreligious moderns, names were bestowed in accordance with ritual, not simply because it may have had a nice ring to it. Joseph and Mary were not stretching themselves out across the hay bales in the stable saying – Je-sus. I like the sound of that. J like Joseph with that hard E sound at the beginning and a soft U at the end, and it fits so well with the last name Of Nazareth – no, names were not like that. They were part of the ritual. Part of the religion. And not only was Jesus circumcised and named according to what was required, but as the firstborn son, he had to be brought to the temple in Jerusalem in order to be presented, or dedicated, to the Lord. Another ritual. But that could not happen until Mary, who after just having a baby was considered ceremonially unclean, had to be properly purified for the duration of time that the law required. (Luke 2.22-23) So then, once purified and after yet another ritual was performed, that of offering two pigeons unto the Lord, (Luke 2.24) they could finally bring little Jesus for dedication. Oh, those troublesome rituals!

    Consider the only account we have of Jesus as a boy. Joseph and Mary went "up to Jerusalem according to the custom of the feast" as our good doctor is so careful to note, where they accidentally left the Son of God behind afterwards. They headed home without him. It took them a whole day to even notice. But like good parents, after realizing their firstborn was missing from the family caravan, they retraced their steps only to find him making himself at home in the temple, talking theology with the professors. And what were they discussing? They were discussing rituals of course. What else was there to discuss? He was sitting amongst the teachers talking about religious ceremonies and the meaning behind them. (1)

Then Jesus grew up. He ventured into the wilderness to meet this man named John. John was going about instructing Jews to repent, and those who would listen were confessing their sins and partaking in an old purification ritual administered by John. It was called baptism. It was nothing new. All the Jews knew about it. It was a ceremonial washing. It taught the people that in order to be on right terms with God that which is unclean must first be made clean. John was teaching them that they must repent and be washed because the kingdom of Heaven was at hand. Into this wilderness world steps Jesus. Jesus wants to be baptized. John hesitates. Jesus insists. John knows full well who this Jesus is, and he is quite certain that he is utterly unworthy to baptize such a man of God. In fact, it is Jesus who should be baptizing John. So John questions. Jesus insists and John relents. Jesus is baptized. He partakes in the ceremonial cleansing. But why? Jesus says why. It must be done to "fulfill all righteousness" (Matt. 3:15) – to fulfill a ritual.

Before moving forward with this righteousness business, let's take a step back for a moment and reflect upon the non-reasons for Jesus' baptism. He was not baptized because he was unclean and needed to be made clean. This should be perfectly obvious to just about anyone. He was not repenting of his sins. He did not have any sins of which to repent. Furthermore, Jesus was not baptized as an example for us to follow. There were a great many other things that Jesus did which were not intended for us to follow, including fasting forty days in the wilderness to be tempted by the devil, that very thing he would immediately do after his baptism. No, Jesus was not merely showing the way. Neither was he publicly proclaiming his faith in God. That Jesus had faith in his Father is not in question, but his reason for being baptized was not to demonstrate that fact. Actually, he was already a member of the household of God by virtue of his being born into the house of Israel and having that birthright sanctified by his circumcision on the eighth day. No, there were definite reasons for Jesus insisting upon his baptism, but these were not them.

The first reason for his baptism was that Jesus was about to be anointed as the high priest over his people. It was part of the ritual for the high priest to wash himself with water before performing certain duties. (2) By receiving baptism, Jesus was demonstrating that he was taking upon himself that ministry. Secondly, although Jesus had zero need of cleansing from sin, the Scriptures tell us that he who knew no sin became sin for us. (2 Cor. 5.21) In his baptism, Jesus was beginning to bear the burden of fallen humanity. Jesus was beginning his ministry of substitution. Both of these reasons have a great deal to do with fulfilling all righteousness. The righteousness of God is found abundantly in his acts of deliverance, and Jesus was embarking upon such a wonderful adventure in deliverance. But there is another reason, a reason even closer to the heart of ritual. Jesus, who was circumcised upon the eighth day according to the law, was now coming to the waters of baptism to show, upon his initiation as our high priest, that the covenant sign was in transition. Soon, circumcision would no longer be required for covenant faithfulness, but rather, baptism. Although the priestly work of deliverance is present in his baptism, to "fulfill all righteousness" is found to an even larger extent in faithful keeping of the covenant. The covenant sign is so closely connected with the covenant promises and obligations that the sign is even referred to as the covenant itself. (Gen. 17.10) What Jesus was doing there in the waters of the Jordan was changing the covenant sign. Don't think for a moment that he was changing the nature of the covenant. He was doing no such thing. He was only changing its sign. The covenant was the same covenant communicated to Abraham centuries earlier, even to Adam and his son Abel. Jesus was changing the sign because he was making the covenant better – not different – just better. The fulfillment of the ritual as it is fulfilled and dispensed through Jesus Christ is what we call the new covenant. It is the new covenant only so far as it is in his blood. It is better because Jesus kept it for us. Christ was simply doing what you would expect the head of humanity to do if he was called upon to consecrate his religion by his own blood.

This is the religion that Jesus was born into. This is how he was raised. This is what he was taught. In this way, he was no different from any other Jew. His life was adorned by ritual. And not once during his life upon this earth did he ever fight against it. Sure, he fought the abuses, but he never fought the ritual. Ritual is part of religion.

Religion. What a nasty little word. A word so nasty that we would be perfectly content to remove it from our Christian dictionaries altogether. After all, the word religion belongs to cults and legalistic sects. Religion means following rules to make God like us. It means working our way into Heaven. Right? Certainly Christianity could not possibly be a religion, could it? Certainly, it's a relationship. Yes, that's it. Relationship. The word relationship sounds so much friendlier, so much more full of…well…love.

I have been guilty of thinking this way myself. When I was a teenager, I would tell this to my peers when they would ask. It was my way of being a witness for Christ. They would say something negative about the Christian religion and I would counter with "Christianity is not a religion; it's a relationship," as if that solved the whole problem. That was my way of doing apologetics. My defense of Christianity was that it was unique not so much in its teachings but in its lack of teachings. I suppose what I meant by the statement was that Christianity is not about doing certain things but rather about encountering a certain person. What I failed to consider was that if Christianity is about encountering Christ, what would the ramifications of such an encounter be if not to be doing certain things?

That Christianity involves a relationship is quite true, but what kind of a relationship is it? Father to child? Friend to friend? Master to servant? Teacher to pupil? Potter to clay? Certainly all of these and more! But is there no system in place? Is there no organization? No authority? No membership laws? No ritual?

The truth is that although Christianity involves a relationship, it is so much more than that, so much greater. It is a relationship built upon the concept of covenant. In it, God agrees – no, more than agrees – God promises to extend certain benefits to us meanwhile binding us to himself by those very promises, henceforth expecting from us, in return, faithfulness to the life he requires. Certainly that is not the kind of relationship I meant when I spoke to my teenage counterparts about Christianity so many years ago. Christianity involves more than relationship. It is a religion because it is a system of faith which requires a matter of practice. Even more so, it is a religion because it is so highly religious. If encountering the living, almighty God is not a religious experience that requires an appropriate response, what is it? If that relationship does not cast us upon our knees in ritual, what does? The Christian religion is a unique religion not because it fails to be religious, but rather because it presents true and unique teachings and true and unique living. Christianity is in no way less religious than any other religion, but on the contrary; it is more religious than all other religions, and for that matter all other relationships, simply because it requires more practice.

Again, baptism is at the very least a ritual. It is part of the religious ceremony of the church. It is a naming rite. It is taking this person, this one who will be called Christian, and setting that one apart unto the Lord. It is making a distinction between what is holy and what is unholy, between what is of Christ and what is of the world. A household set apart unto God is a religious household, and a religious household cannot practice their religion without some form of ritual.

Knowing, therefore, that baptism is at the very least a ritual of the Christian religion, it is essential to recognize that it is certainly far more than that. The 'more than that' will be dealt with in subsequent pages. The problem I see, however, is that there are many in the evangelical Christian community, maybe half at least, who understand baptism to be more like a Baby on Board sign. If we come across a car with this sign in the window, we assume, though we cannot be sure, that there is a baby inside. What does that do for us? Besides making us wonder if the sign is true, it might, maybe, remind us to drive a little more carefully, but nothing more. But what does it do for the baby? On a certain level, it identifies the baby with the car, granted. To hit the car might mean injuring the baby. But it does not follow that hitting the baby will injure the car. The sign is out there for all to see. Will it protect the baby, given a collision? Essentially, the sign means nothing to the baby. It is merely a sign. It makes a statement, nothing more. It says nothing whatever about how the baby got in the car, nor whether or not the baby will remain in the car. There is no meaning behind the sign other than to say 'Baby on Board'. It tells us nothing about either the baby or the car. That is why we begin to invent various rituals of our own like dry baby dedications, personal testimonies, and altar calls. Christians really do long for ritual. If only they might see that the ritual is already there. So the problem, then, is that those with the sign-only, or Baby on Board mindset regarding baptism not only fail to acknowledge the 'more than that' on the subject, but they fail to acknowledge the very minimal meaning as well, that baptism is a religious rite, a ceremonial cleansing of Jewish heritage and custom.

It is important to note at the outset of a discussion on baptism that Jesus did not come to do away with the system of ritual of which the Jews had been accustomed for over a thousand years. Rather, as he testified himself, he came not to abolish the law but to fulfill it. (Matt. 5:17) He came to simplify the ritual. To compact it. He did not come to set up a different religion. He came to make perfect the very religion that he was born into. The same God. The same covenant. The same expectations. Jesus came as a revelation of those things. The Jews were not faulted for failing to embrace a new religion. On the contrary, they were faulted for failing to understand their own. Jesus came to take all the ritual of which they had been acquainted, all that meaning and tedious observance, and he packaged it within his own person. As a result, he gave us sacraments.

2
A SACRAMENT

To say that baptism is a ceremonial cleansing is really saying two separate things about the subject. If we admit that baptism is ceremonial then we are essentially admitting that it is symbolic. If we left it at that, then we would call baptism a sign, which of course it is. But if we left it at that, then baptism would be considered a mere sign, which it certainly is not. To admit that baptism is mere ceremony should make the Baby on Board crowd quite content being that ceremony by itself changes absolutely nothing. But baptism is not like this. Baptism under this age of fulfillment changes things a great deal. That is why we should also refer to it as a cleansing, or a washing. When Aaron, for example, washed himself before entering the holy place, he was playing a part. He was acting. He was doing something symbolic which pointed to a greater reality. The washing may have made his body clean, but it left his heart at the mercy of God. There was no power in or through the water to actually purify him of sin. It was a teaching tool more or less, but one of enormous importance to God. That is what has changed under Christ. Under the fulfillment of Christ, ceremony is no longer acting. It is living. Christ is the reality to which all the symbols pointed. Therefore, a Christian does not need to wash himself before entering the sanctuary. A Christian need not even enter the sanctuary at all. Christ has already gone ahead into the Holy of Holies. (Heb. 9:12) We have been given all of that by Christ's fulfillment of ritual.

But baptism is still a cleansing. It is not mere ceremony, but rather, ceremonial cleansing. Though many would prefer to shy away from the concept of ceremony, there are still many who are adamant that baptism is nothing more than ceremony, nothing more than symbolism, a simple outward sign pointing to an inward reality, and it certainly is that – but not merely that. That mere sign has been done away with, fulfilled in Christ. Those who are adamant that baptism is a mere sign have inserted themselves into a time and place which is no longer applicable, the time and place of Aaron, for instance. Mere signs have become obsolete.

    We call baptism a ceremonial cleansing because it is both a real ceremony as well as real cleansing. It is not pretend. Baptism washes – no, not by the power of the water – but by the power of God. How can that be? Because baptism is a sacrament.

    A sacrament is a physical element, a sign or symbol if you will, around which Heaven and Earth collide. A sacrament is like a portal. The elements have no power in themselves, but God uses them to communicate something significant about himself in an earthly manner that can be grasped. It is quite different than God speaking through his written Word. The Word is believed through the ears. But God did not give us ears only. He gave us eyes and fingers and a nose and tongue. He has chosen to reveal himself to us through all of our senses. A sacrament is the reality of God captured by contact with the portal itself.

    It should be nothing too strange to speak this way, for this is normal operations in God's playbook. Under normal circumstances, which, in other words, means almost every circumstance, God reveals himself to humanity through physical elements like, for instance, bread, wine, water, and a man named Jesus. Is it too strange to think of Jesus as sacramental? Why should it be? Of course he is! God could choose to speak to us directly if he wished. He could communicate to us Spirit to spirit, without words, without signs, by simple understanding if he so desired. But that is not normal. Even the written word is something tangible. God uses physical means to communicate and reveal himself to his people. When those means are instituted by Christ as a ritual, then it is called a sacrament.

Take, for instance, the historical teaching of Rome regarding the sacraments: "Sacraments are 'powers that come forth' from the Body of Christ, which is ever living and life giving. They are actions of the Holy Spirit at work in his Body, the Church. They are the 'masterworks of God' in the new and everlasting covenant."(1)

Read that again. Notice how close an association exists between the Body of Christ and his Body the Church. The sacraments are said to be the workings of the Holy Spirit, bringing the life-giving power of Christ himself upon his church, or in other words, upon his body. The church, being the body of Christ, is sustained by Christ himself through the dispensing of the Holy Spirit in sacraments.

In case the already mentioned definition of sacraments is too popish for your taste, consider the words of the Westminster Assembly: "A sacrament is a holy ordinance instituted by Christ, wherein, by sensible signs, Christ, and the benefits of the new covenant, are represented, sealed, and applied to believers."(2)

Think about that for a moment. A sacrament is not merely an ordinance, but a holy ordinance. A sacrament is not merely a sign, but a sign by which Christ himself is applied to believers. It is not as though a sacrament is a sign which points to Christ from somewhere in the distance, it is the vehicle that brings Christ to us so that we may be close. It is not a sign stuck to the window of the car which reads 'Baby on Board', but more like the car itself which carries the baby and keeps her near the parent.

Furthermore, the Westminster divines noted that "There is, in every sacrament, a spiritual relation, or sacramental union, between the sign and the thing signified: whence it comes to pass, that the names and effects of the one are attributed to the other."(3)

What is this 'spiritual relation', this 'sacramental union'? First of all, it does *not* mean that by the sacrament there is union between the *recipient* of the sign and the thing signified. That would mean that by virtue of the sign, the partaker of the sign automatically is joined together with the meaning of the sign. There is no ipso facto union taking place meaning that by the mere fact of the application of water the recipient is automatically joined to Christ. It is more subtle than that, yet no less real. It means that the sign is joined together, in a sacramental union, or by covenant so to speak, with the thing signified. In other words, in baptism, the water is in union with the regenerating work of the Holy Spirit, so much so that the terms may be used interchangeably; for example, the term 'receiving baptism' becomes synonymous with the term 'receiving the Holy Spirit', and therefore because the sacrament (the sign) is joined together with the Holy Spirit (the thing signified), we may rightly say that by virtue of receiving the sacrament, we have also received the Holy Spirit.

But the Westminster Assembly was full of crotchety puritans, and naturally, as a result they gave us a crotchety and verbose confession. Certainly, there must be other, less stuffy opinions. We will spend more time next chapter in comparing the various confessions of the church in the matter of baptism, but as far as the nature of a sacrament in general is concerned, let's ask the less verbose Book of Common Prayer. In it we read: "The sacraments are outward and visible signs of inward and spiritual grace, given by Christ as sure and certain means by which we receive that grace."(4)

Baptism is like this. Baptism is an outward sign, hence the washing with water, of an inward grace, hence the cleansing of God. But baptism is not that only. It is a sure means, or a testimony, that God's grace is real and present. It is not only a finger that points, but a hand that holds. Baptism is a sacrament, a holy ordinance given by Christ for the awakening of his people unto himself, for the sanctification of his children, for a sure and certain testimony that God is real and present within the life of his church. Baptism does these things. It is the life giving power of God in visible form. But don't take my word for it. Listen instead to the apostle, Paul, in his letter to the Galatians:

"For you are all sons of God through faith in Christ Jesus. For as many of you who were baptized into Christ have put on Christ." (Gal. 3:26-27)

Is baptism not a sacrament in the mind of Paul? The great apostle has just finished rebuking the Galatians for attempting justification by ritual. Paul assures them that justification comes not by law but by promise. Therefore, the only way of receiving this promise is by faith in Christ, for Christ alone is the confirmation of the covenant; he is the one in whom all fulfillment of ritual is found, so that once faith has been confirmed by the Christ of the covenant, the types and shadows of the ritual fall away, like the peeling of an orange, so the fruit itself remains.

And what does the apostle say about this baptism, this ceremonial washing? He says it is the putting on of Christ. "For as many of you who were baptized into Christ have put on Christ." He says it is union. He says it is synonymous with faith. According to the apostle, faith in Christ is the means of being made sons of God. According to the apostle, baptism is the means of putting him on, of wearing him about. Baptism and faith do the same thing in the mind of Paul, but they do not do the same thing apart from one another. It is not as if you can take the baptism and discard the faith or take the faith and say fiddlesticks to the baptism. They are essential means of receiving Christ. And therefore, "You are all one in Christ Jesus. And if you are Christ's, then you are Abraham's seed and heirs according to the promise." (Gal. 3:29)

Amazing! Notice how the apostle returns to the old. He does not say that those who are Abraham's seed are Christ's but on the contrary – those who are Christ's are Abraham's seed. Those who are made new have access to what is old. Again the only thing new is that Christ has come. He has made the old signs obsolete. He has turned baptism into a new sign – but not a sign only, a sacrament – for it is through baptism that the fullness is received. And look at the unity! It is through common baptism that we are one in Christ, *not* through common profession, as if there is a difference.

Another example is Paul writing to the Romans about dying to sin and living for Christ. He mentions a great deal about this in chapter six, but it is what he does *not* say that may be even more telling.

We should avoid sin because we died to sin. We died to sin because Christ died *for* our sins. This is true, but this is not what the apostle says. Sure, he could have left it at that. He could have continued by saying that we should avoid sin because we have not only been united to Christ in his death but also in his resurrection. He could have gone on to say that this union takes place by faith, and because we have faith in Christ, we can be assured that the old man has died and that the new man lives. Therefore, since we have died to sin in our union with Christ, we are now free from sin by the power of his resurrection. He could have gone on and on and on, and for the most part he does, but not in that way. In fact, he fails to mention that little word 'faith' even once in the entire body of chapter six. Of course, faith is assumed, but it is not referred to at all, nor is it even whispered about. What is mentioned, then? What is given as the vehicle of this union in death and life? What is given as the reason to avoid sin if not faith?

It is baptism. "Or do you not know that as many of us as were baptized into Christ were baptized into His death? Therefore, we were buried with Him through baptism into death, that just as Christ was raised from the dead by the glory of the Father, even so we should walk in newness of life." (Rom. 6:3-4) According to Paul, it is baptism that unites us. According to Paul, it is baptism that does something. According to Paul, it is because of baptism that we do not let sin reign in our mortal bodies that we should obey it in its lusts because it is baptism that proves to us that sin shall not have dominion over us for we are not under law but under grace. We cannot spiritualize this. We cannot pretend it was never written. We cannot try and drain all of the meaning out by saying that his point is about the mode, because if we do, we would be admitting more ritual than we may have ever dared imagine, for we would be saying essentially that by going down into the water we are united with Christ in death and by coming up out of the water we are united with him in resurrection, ipso facto, in the actual moment of the administration of it. No, not many dare to say this much. But there is still much to be said. Baptism is the sacrament which unites us to Christ so that we belong to him as opposed to belonging to sin. We obey Christ, not sin. We live for Christ, not sin. Paul is about union, not mode! Baptism is about union, real union, not a finger pointing, but a hand holding.

Sacraments, therefore, are life giving metaphors. They bring Christ to bear upon us. They are terrible and wonderful, frightening and alive. They are means of grace. But there are those, as we will see later, who do not believe in sacraments. They are confident they don't exist. They believe in them about as much as they believe in fairy tales, and they are those who could not imagine how God can really speak to man by a common loaf of bread or a cup of wine or a douse of water – or a common ass, for that matter. Remember, unity is at stake.

3

A COMMONALITY OF CONFESSION

I do not wish to get caught up in semantics, and I hope I will avoid bogging you down with trivialities. I only wish to make a passionate plea for what seems to me as plain as the nose on my face, though I admit my nose is really not so plain to me unless I am looking in the mirror. So let us realize that although I wish to avoid what might appear as technicalities, I will not be able to make such a passionate plea unless I am first gazing into the mirror of God's Word, a mirror which certainly points to many theological warts and blemishes, but a mirror without which understanding baptism would be an impossible task. But then again, is that not what baptism communicates? – Our warts and blemishes? And how they must be purified by God himself if we are to ever have communion with him? If I am able to prove anything at all, I hope it should be that baptism is grace.

With that being said, I have full intention of facing the Scriptures head on, for I think that on the subject of baptism, Scripture has too often taken a back seat to theological reasoning, though I understand how. I hope to maintain a clear path through the Scriptures and will most certainly be drawing upon the Word of God as the authority behind this discussion, but with the Word of God at the forefront, there will be a few more technicalities to address, if indeed they can be called technicalities, for in many ways they are like a light in the fog. They are the confessions of the church. They might seem like technicalities, but they are quite necessary. By looking at them, we will be able to appreciate a long standing consensus in the area of baptism despite the fragmentation of the church. Before we plunge deeper into the waters of baptism, however, let us recount the characteristics of a sacrament.

First of all, a sacrament is a holy ordinance instituted by Christ. Secondly, a sacrament is a sign and a seal of something. That something will be determined later on. Next, a sacrament is attached to the promises of God's grace. Furthermore, it not only communicates that grace, but it serves as a means of receiving that grace. Finally, it acts as a witness, or a type of confirmation of our union with Christ.

These are the general ideas on the sacraments taken from the understanding born out of the Reformation, an understanding held, surprisingly, in close commonality among the Lutherans, Presbyterians, Reformed, Anglicans, and Episcopalians. There is much unity, to be sure. Unfortunately, as simple observation shows us, those somewhat uniform groups probably make up only half the population of the evangelical church. But anyhow, knowing that there is a common understanding of what a sacrament is, let us turn our attention to the ways in which these traditions understand baptism itself.

Remember, Christianity is very much a religion. One reason for this is that it contains a system of belief. It contains doctrines. It contains information about God himself, or revelations to put it more accurately. God expects these revelations to be believed because they are the foundations of his religion. So Christianity is about believing something very specific, something extraordinary, yet at the same time as common as a butterfly or a mountain. God has spoken, and his Word has been preserved for us all to hear. The purpose of a confession, then, is to take the teachings of the Scriptures and categorize them into a theology. Confessions are not meant to supplant the Scriptures. They are simply the teachings of the Scriptures organized into a doctrine of faith. They are an interpretation of the Scriptures.

A Confession of Faith is like a grocery store. Inside the store is an enormous amount of food and other necessities. But they are organized into categories to make shopping easier. How would it be if you went to the grocery store and the ground beef was next to the diapers and the spare ribs were next to the pepper, if the pork chops were with the eggs and the ham with the ice cream? Just as a grocery store organizes its products into categories such as meats, dairy, produce, and frozen foods, so a Confession of Faith organizes the teachings of Scripture into categories such as creation, justification, law, sacraments, and many more. The various confessions of the church help formulate the revelation of God for at least two necessary reasons:

The first reason is that the church has been commissioned by God to hold and guard the truth he has revealed. (1 Tim. 3:15) God's truth has been entrusted to the church. It is the church's privilege – not only privilege – but duty to maintain purity in doctrine, and this task is impossible in the hands of insane men. The insanity of mankind gives birth to all kinds of ill-conceived doctrines, all sorts of fantastical theologies, and a myriad of imaginary teachings. That is the danger of placing the Scriptures into the hands of commoners, and by commoners I mean human beings. But that is also the beauty. If God wanted us to have the entire Scriptures already systematized, he would have given them to us the way he gave the law to Moses, precise and written on stone. But most of the Word of God is organic, growing out from the seeds of the earth as men live and move and have their being, and organic things are usually messy. The Confessions of Faith are the result of learned men of God standing up in the face of the messiness of circumstances in their lives in different times and different places, and pulling together in unity against their adversaries, often in the midst of persecution. Confessions of Faith are declarations of the truths of God. It is as if to say, 'All teachings are not equal. There is truth and there is error. Here is the best summary of the truth, the best summary of God's Word that we can devise.' Confessions of Faith are pleas for unity.

So with unity of truth being the first reason for the necessity of confessions, the second is like it. They are important for maintaining truth and defending it against error. Don't forget. Christianity is a religion. It involves a system of belief called faith which is the foundation of life which is called practice. Therefore, Confessions of Faith to some degree keep churches accountable to the teachings of Scripture. They are not a substitute for Scripture, but a gauge. After all, if the church taught one thing for two hundred years, it should make us uneasy if it suddenly began teaching something else altogether. The confessions help control the injustice of mad men leading other men mad.

But enough of this already! I am not so interested, concerning our present topic, in defending the need for confessions as I am in explaining what they have to teach us as to what baptism is, and furthermore to show the astonishing commonality among many predominant, yet separate denominations of Christianity in this area. What has the church said about baptism for the last five hundred years?

Let us begin with maybe the simplest yet most shocking of the lot, the Augsburg Confession of the Lutheran Church which reads: "…our churches teach that baptism is necessary for salvation and that God's grace is offered through baptism."[1]

What is the matter with these people? Haven't they ever heard of justification by faith alone? Of course they have. They're Lutherans, after all. But where do they get the nerve to suggest that baptism is necessary for salvation? Because they probably read Mark 16:16. Notice the Lutherans are *not* saying baptism is *sufficient* for salvation, only necessary. Baptism and faith are not contraries. They are different elements of the salvation experience. They are both necessary. The question then becomes, necessary in what way? What do they do? Well, that will hopefully be answered in the pages of this book. But consider, do the Scriptures ever indicate that *faith* is sufficient for our salvation? I think James would take exception to that notion. This statement in the Augsburg is simple because it is brief and pointed. It is shocking because it flies in the face of our precious understanding of faith alone. Or does it? Is it really that different than the other confessions? Let's ask Heinrich Bullinger, primary architect of the 2nd Helvetic Confession:

"Now to be baptized in the name of Christ is to be enrolled, entered, and received into the covenant and family, and so into the inheritance of the sons of God; yes, and in this life to be called after the name of God; that is to say, to be called a son of God; to be cleansed also from the filthiness of sins, and to be granted the manifold grace of God, in order to lead a new and innocent life."(2)

Is this not in general agreement with the Augsburg? Does this not demonstrate in greater detail the reasons associated with calling baptism "necessary for salvation"? According to the 2nd Helvetic Confession, by baptism, the recipient is adopted into God's family and called a son of God, washed clean from sin, and granted grace for newness of life. This is what the Reformed churches of Europe taught for centuries. This is rarely what the Reformed churches of today care to remember. Take, for example, the teaching of the Thirty Nine Articles of Religion:

"Baptism is not only a sign of profession, and mark of difference, whereby Christian men are discerned from others that be not christened, but it is also a sign of Regeneration or New-Birth, whereby, as by an instrument, they that receive Baptism rightly are grafted into the Church; the promises of the forgiveness of sin, and of our adoption to be the sons of God by the Holy Ghost, are visibly signed and sealed, Faith is confirmed, and Grace increased by virtue of prayer unto God."(3)

Or, in the words of the Westminster Family:

"Baptism is a sacrament of the New Testament, ordained by Jesus Christ, not only for the solemn admission of the party baptized into the visible Church; but also to be unto him a sign and seal of the covenant of grace, of his ingrafting into Christ, of regeneration, of remission of sins, and of his giving up unto God, through Jesus Christ, to walk in the newness of life. Which sacrament is, by Christ's own appointment, to be continued in His Church until the end of the world."(4)

We have heard, in part, from the Lutherans, the Reformed, the Anglicans/Episcopalians, and the Presbyterians. For another angle, let's add the confessional statement of the United Methodists, a group who is no less historically significant, but generally considered less confessional:

"We believe the Sacraments, ordained by Christ, are symbols and pledges of the Christian's profession and of God's love toward us. They are means of grace by which God works invisibly in us, quickening, strengthening and confirming our faith in him…We believe Baptism signifies entrance into the household of faith, and is a symbol of repentance and inner cleansing from sin, a representation of the new birth in Christ Jesus and a mark of Christian discipleship."(5)

Is there not significant commonality among the historic denominations? Is there not substantial unity among these Christian traditions? Is there not similar understandings? Certainly there is! These branches of the church share in common a sacramental understanding of baptism, and consequently, each of these branches of the church bring their children to the waters of baptism as well.

If you take the time to investigate these historic confessions, even in further depth than you have been given here, you will notice the common threads which run throughout, primarily: 1) That baptism is a sacrament of the church, 2) That baptism is a rite of admittance into the church body, 3) That baptism is a sign and a seal, or means, of receiving God's grace and redemptive work on behalf of his people, 4) That baptism communicates the promises of forgiveness, adoption, and regeneration, 5) That baptism serves as a means to assurance of salvation, and 6) That baptism obligates the recipient to walk in newness of life.

These are no small matters. The fact that God uses baptism to really do something to and for the recipient is of great importance to our understanding of the gospel of grace. These traditions are no small sample. These are the majority of predominant branches of Christianity since the time of the Reformation. They are furthermore consistent with what the church has taught from the beginning, even in accordance with the Nicene Creed of the fourth century in which "We acknowledge one baptism for the remission of sins." Is it not time to re-evaluate our teachings concerning baptism and return to the confessions of our faith? Is it not time to return to baptism as a sacrament? As a means of grace? For in the same way that faith is a carrier of the benefits of grace and redemption, so the sacraments are carriers of the promises of that grace. They are confirmations that God will really do what he has promised to do and those promises are really for me. Consider the following words of Luther in his Small Catechism:

"Baptism is not simple water only, but it is the water included in God's command and connected with God's Word...It works forgiveness of sins, delivers from death and the devil, and gives eternal salvation to all who believe this, as the words and promises of God declare."

"How can water do such great things?"

"It is not the water indeed that does them, but the Word of God, which is in and with the water, and faith, which trusts this

Word of God in the water. For without the Word of God, the water is simple water and no Baptism. But with the Word of God it is a Baptism, that is a gracious water of life and a washing of regeneration in the Holy Spirit."(6)

These teaching are probably new to some of you, probably not to others, but either way I encourage you to read carefully these confessions which were born out of the Protestant Reformation. These are strong words which place a rather high view on the power of a religious ritual. Think about them and about how this has been the teaching of the churches for centuries.

But what about the Bible? Show me in God's word! Patience, please. My intention in this chapter is to show that, although the church has been uprooted and divided in so many unfortunate ways and in so many trying circumstances, there has remained, in most denominations, a unity about who is to be admitted into the church body and the means in which this is to occur. The unity has remained in the teaching that baptism, as a sacrament, is the sacrament of church membership, and furthermore, though I have not thus far touched upon infant baptism as a topic in the confessions, I will do so now in conclusion with the words of the Belgic Confession concerning children and baptism:

"And truly, Christ has shed his blood no less for washing the little children of believers than he did for adults. Therefore they ought to receive the sign and sacrament of what Christ has done for them, just as the Lord commanded in the law that by offering a lamb for them the sacrament of the suffering and death of Christ would be granted them shortly after their birth. This was the sacrament of Jesus Christ."(7)

4
THE DISSENTING VIEW

Despite the commonality of confession which exists within the church in the area of baptism, there exists alongside of it a large, to put it mildly, dissenting opinion regarding the nature of baptism and its rightful recipients. In the dissenting view, baptism is not a sacrament. It is symbolic only, like the Baby on Board sign or the Scarlett Letter. It is informative only. This is the case with the dissenting view. The recipient of baptism is informing the witnesses of the baptism that God has given him grace, that he has repented of his sins, and that he wants to follow Christ. It is a public proclamation of his faith. He is publically proclaiming that he has been united to Christ's death and resurrection by faith – that he is now a Christian. It is identification with Christ only in the sense that it points toward a work that God has already done in the recipient. It is the first step, and if not the first step than an important step, in a show of repentance. It is a God on Board sign.

This is the view held by Baptists; Pentecostals; Anabaptists such as Amish, Mennonite and Brethren; and most non-denominational churches, para-denominational churches, and parachurch organizations. I will call this perspective baptistic as opposed to sacramental. In this view, the only worthy recipients of baptism are those who have cognitively embraced the gospel, coherently articulated the gospel to whatever standard is deemed appropriate, and have committed their lives to Christ. Only then can they receive the waters of baptism.

Now I am certain to have some of my baptistic readers throwing their hands up into the air in frustration. "You've got it all wrong! That's not right! That's not exactly what we believe!

You're not being fair!" Well, I'm trying to be as fair and accurate as possible, and as one who was raised in baptistic churches, I am familiar with their essential teachings on baptism. The baptistic understanding of baptism is that in every case it may only be administered *after* the recipient has come to faith and repentance because it is impossible for anyone to truly identify with Christ unless he has first come to know Christ in a saving manner. You may only rightly receive baptism *after* you are saved, and if for some reason you accidentally receive baptism *before* getting saved, it is often said to be no real baptism at all. To clarify matters, let's just say that in the baptistic perspective, baptism must never precede justification. Well, that, and also that baptism is not a sacrament. But let's let the Baptists speak for themselves. Some of them have their own confessions, by the way, the following being taken from the London Baptist Confession of Faith:

"Baptism and the Lord's Supper are ordinances of positive and sovereign institution, appointed by the Lord Jesus, the only lawgiver, to be continued in His Church to the end of the world...Baptism is an ordinance of the New Testament, ordained by Jesus Christ, to be to the person who is baptized – a sign of his fellowship with Christ in His death and resurrection; of his being engrafted into Christ; of remission of sins; and of that person's giving up of himself to God, through Jesus Christ, to live and walk in newness of life. Those who actually profess repentance towards God, faith in, and obedience to, our Lord Jesus Christ, are the only proper subjects for this ordinance."(1)

Notice that in the baptistic description, baptism is said to be an ordinance. Agreed. But what little word is missing that was included in the Westminster Confession of Faith, that little word which makes such a great difference? Holy. In the baptistic world, baptism is not holy. It is not a holy ordinance. It is not sanctified by God. The recipient supposedly is, but not the ordinance. A holy person is being washed with unholy water in an unholy ceremony usually on a holy day appointed by a holy God who has not sanctified the ordinance. He has sanctioned it, just not sanctified it. I suppose baptism is common, then, as common as bathwater or the rain that falls from the sky. But do not pay too much mind to the omission of that little word, for the omission is only meant to imply that the ordinance is not a sacrament. If baptism was a sacrament, it would be holy, but because it is not a sacrament, it is common. It is no more holy than the church organ.

Some of you might wonder, "What's the big deal? Is it really worth splitting hairs over whether or not baptism is a holy ordinance?" Sadly, the hairs have already been split. If I take my baptized children and try to join a Baptist church, if that Baptist church is thinking straight and cares about their doctrine, once my children have come of age, they will not allow them to join the church until they are baptized once again. Why? Because their original baptism that took place when they were infants is not considered valid. Is this splitting hairs? No, this is more than splitting hairs. This is creating a chasm between two Bible believing Christians. The problem is that too many Christians are content with this chasm. It doesn't bother them. "Let us do things our way and let them do things their way," they say, but when it comes down to actually receiving someone into the fellowship, suddenly a wall is erected. Is this not controversial? If not, I think it should be.

"But," you might respond, "What does placing a prohibition upon infants have to do with whether or not baptism is a holy ordinance? Couldn't a sacramentalist just as well place prohibitions upon baptistic families joining a church unless they consent to baptizing their children?" I think a short answer would be that in the baptistic position, most of the time it is not as if baptism is too holy for the children; rather, the children are not holy enough for baptism. The wall which has been erected is equally tall on both sides. Unity will not be found by knocking the wall down or by pretending that it doesn't exist, but only by coming around onto the other side. Once the church is on the same side, there will be unity. In all practicality, the wall has less to do with the theology of baptism than it does with the theology of children. But remember what the Westminsters said about a sacrament. It is a holy ordinance in which there exists a sacramental union between the sign and the thing signified. This means that if the Baptists are correct, if baptism is not a sacrament, then there is no union taking place between the washing of water and God himself. The act of baptism is actually taking place apart from any sanctifying work of the Holy Spirit. Therefore, when it comes to a matter of practice, and when the emphasis is placed upon man's response to God's work instead upon the holiness of God's work, it becomes easy to see how certain people might not be deemed worthy participants by virtue of their lack of response.

More will be said about children in Part III of this book, but for now, it is sufficient to note how the Baptists differ from the sacramentalists in that the Baptists, particularly modern Baptists, do not treat baptism as a holy ordinance. It is not a sacrament. It is in this way that they have dissented from the historic position.

Once again, maybe those of the baptistic persuasion are quite content with that. Let's look at another word which has been omitted from the definition – the word 'seal'. Notice how the Westminsters insist that baptism is not only a sign, but a seal as well. It is both a sign *and* a seal of a covenant. The Londoners say not so fast. They don't believe that baptism seals anything, because if it did, if baptism was a sign that also sealed a certain deal, then it would imply some sort of power that has been vested into the sign, much like a signature on a contract, or even more so, like the signet ring of a king, signing and sealing an edict, and Baptists apparently do not believe in that sort of thing when it comes to the ordinances and edicts of the King of Kings. The omission of the word 'seal' is purposeful in the same manner as the omission of the word 'holy'.

The Londoners do not want the ordinance of baptism to be confused in any way with a sacrament.

No, on the contrary, they are happy with baptism being called a sign because signs don't do anything, and the Londoners, who are very much devoted to the sovereign power of God in salvation, do not want anyone to get the false impression that it is the water and not God which possesses the powers in converting death to life. That is why they insist that as far as the sign is concerned, it must be a sign of something that has already occurred, like a finger pointing rather than a hand holding. It is certainly admirable as far as protecting the reputation of God is concerned, but let's be careful not to protect him in areas where he desires no protection. If God wants his powers dispensed through a water ritual, then by all means let him, the risk of confusion notwithstanding.

Now, the London Baptist position is similar to the Westminster position in that it shares some of the same language such as 'engrafting into Christ', 'remission of sins', and 'giving up unto God to walk in newness of life', though there is no mention of regeneration nor, surprisingly, admission into the visible church. Though the Baptist position shares similar language, the great difference is that Baptists assume that all the aforementioned benefits are already present in the recipient *before* the act of baptism. In other words, engrafting, forgiveness, walking in newness of life, and for that matter regeneration are not promises attached to the act of baptism, but rather a condition *for* baptism. Consequently, the act of baptism becomes, more or less, a personal testimony and nothing more.

Let's think for a moment about the implications of this dissenting viewpoint. First, if baptism is not a sacrament, then there is no union taking place between the water and the Holy Spirit. I think the baptistic minded folks would be content with that, but we should understand that in that case there are no spiritual benefits received by, nor even offered to, the one being baptized. Therefore, if there are no spiritual benefits being received, there is nothing to seal, and if there is nothing to seal, we can assume that there are no promises attached to the ceremony. If there are no promises attached and nothing is received, then baptism cannot be said to be a means of grace. If baptism is not a means of receiving grace then neither can it give any assurance of grace. Furthermore, if baptism does not unite anything or seal anything or convey anything, then neither does it bind anything, and if it does not bind anything, then neither does it bind *us* to *Christ*. Therefore, if it does not bind us to Christ, it does not obligate us to Christ, for there is no covenant without a seal. So even though it may be a 'sign' for the recipient to 'walk in newness of life', the recipient is not bound to do so, for there is no union which exists binding him to faithfulness. Baptism is a mere testimony – no, less than that – a mere *human* testimony which tells of a prior commitment to walk in newness of life, but without the perpetual obligation to do so. But then again, the baptistic minded folks may be perfectly content with that. The question that should be foremost in our minds, and I am sure it is for most proponents of the dissenting view, is whether or not God's Word is content with that.

  Notice, also, in regard to baptism, the omission of the term, 'covenant' in the aforementioned section of the London Baptist Confession of Faith. Now, the Londoners are very much in tune with the concept of covenant, but instead of recognizing baptism as a sign of covenant, they treat it as if it is a sign of experience. Instead of being a sign of what God has done *in* and *through* Christ, it is thought to be a sign of what God has done in and through the *individual*. It becomes a mark, not of divine faithfulness, but of human response. The concept of covenant is stripped away from the ordinance so that baptism becomes, in essence a profession of a profession, or to put it another way, a sign of a sign.

Actually, it really becomes nothing at all except a formality. But Christ commanded it! Yes, he apparently did command this particular formality. I cannot think of any other examples of Christ exhibiting such fondness for formalities. It seems that Christ usually has reasons for his commands – beneficial reasons. It seems that Christ's commands usually serve a purpose greater than a game of charades. If Adam had not eaten the forbidden fruit he would have lived. If the rich young ruler had gone and sold all he owned and given to the poor he would have reaped treasures in Heaven. There is a correlation between Christ's commands and the fruit of obedience. Christ might push a child into the pond to teach him how to swim, but he doesn't push him into the pond to teach him it's a pond. If baptism does nothing, then why do it? If it does nothing, then why did Christ command it? Wouldn't a public statement of testimony be sufficient without having to get anybody wet?

But again, someone might argue, "You're not being fair. Baptism might be a mere testimony, but it is a powerful testimony. The visual image of someone being dunked under the water and brought back up is much more dramatic than simple words of profession." Yes, that might be true, but in the end it still does nothing more than simple words of profession. If it is impact we want, I would think diving from a fifty foot platform into a small pool of water would add greater impact than a simple dunking would do.

And for some Christian folks, a profession *is* enough. Many churches do not consider baptism important enough, even though Christ has commanded it, as to make certain that all their professing believers even receive baptism (at least once). "After all, isn't my word good enough? Don't you trust me? If I tell you I'm a Christian, then by-God I'm a Christian!"

Just because Christ commanded baptism does not mean that we do it merely because he commanded it. He has commanded it

43

because it is of particular use to him and to us. Notice how the Londoners, under the teaching of baptism and the Lord's Supper, make it a point to remind us that Christ is the "only lawgiver" as if being baptized can be filed away in the same drawer as turning the other cheek. That Christ is the only lawgiver may be true, but it does not follow that baptism should be considered law. If the rich young ruler had given to the poor, he would have reaped treasures in Heaven. That is not the same as saying that if the rich young ruler reaped treasures in Heaven that it would have been because he gave to the poor. Baptism may be a command, but it is not an empty command. It is a command that is always given in the context of obtaining salvation. Repent! is also a command, but we don't call it a law. We don't go around talking about the 'law of repentance' like we go around talking about the 'law of love'. That is because repenting is as much attached to the act of faith as baptism is.

If baptism is not a sacrament, then it is not much of anything. If baptism is a mere ordinance, then it is just *mere*, period. The dissenting view is an empty view. It removes the cleansing from the ceremony. It divorces the religion from the ritual. And yes, as we will see in the following chapter, it internalizes the 'Christ' in Christian.

5
THE CHRISTIAN

Sometimes, when trying to make progress, it is a good idea to take a step back and survey the landscape before continuing to push forward, just to make sure you are headed in the right direction. This is one of those times. It would do us all well if we took a moment, not only in the pages of this book, but in our own lives to consider the often used word that has come to cause so much confusion in our theology. The word is Christian.

What is a Christian? Is it a regular church goer? Is it a nice, decent person? Is it someone who has gotten saved or been slain in the Spirit? Is it someone who has walked the aisle or prayed to receive Jesus as his personal Lord and Savior? Is it someone who gives money to the poor? Is it a republican? A country music artist? A Protestant? A Catholic? Is it someone who wears Bible verses on his t-shirts? Is it all of these, none of these, or something else entirely? I think if you asked that question to ten Christians, you might receive ten different answers. If you broadened the survey to include even those outside the church, you would receive enough variety to open a smorgasbord restaurant. But it wasn't always so. There was a time when the word Christian meant something very specific to a world that was turned upside down by a preachy carpenter and a band of renegade fishermen. There was a time when being called a Christian carried with it significant cultural and political ramifications. There was a time when being called a Christian meant that you were trouble for the Roman Empire. Then there was a time to the contrary when being called a Christian meant that you were a *citizen* of the Roman Empire. In that particular case, it was because the Empire changed, not the Christians. Today, being called a Christian usually means something quite different. It is no longer a threat to much of anything. In fact, it has been managed to the point of keeping it sufficiently enough on the fringe of culture so as not to disrupt the order of the powers of the age. It is tolerated too well and not nearly enough. The manner in which it is different is not so easy for me to put into words. I think I would have to say that, at least in the western world, Christianity is not the same affliction that it used to be. So what has changed?

The problem is that being called a Christian is exactly that – it is something that you are called. And not only that, but it is something that you are called from the outside. Unfortunately, it is the Christians themselves who have confused the issue by insisting that if being a Christian is something that you are called at all, it is something that you are called on the inside. If it is recognized as a label at all, then it is a self-imposed label. It has become more subtle than it once was. More introspective. Almost more dishonest. Being a Christian has become invisible in many respects. Invisible and intangible. Becoming a Christian is now thought to be something that happens to you in the salvation process. It has become synonymous with 'being saved'. It has lost much of its cultural and political significance. In fact, God forbid, sometimes I can be a Christian even if I am the only one in the entire world who knows it. Being a Christian in our current cultural climate has become something almost entirely subjective.

But it was not always so. 'Christian' is a title at one time given to those who followed Jesus as the Christ. The Christians did not give this title to themselves. It was placed upon them by the outsiders, by the world. We are told that the disciples of Christ were first called Christians in Antioch. (Acts 11.26) We are also told that if anyone suffers as a Christian then he should glory in God. (1 Pet. 4.16) The label 'Christian' was not an endearing label by any means, at least not at first. It was a label of contempt and ridicule.

Being a Christian meant that you acknowledged that Jesus Christ was raised from the dead and lived your life according to the revolutionary implications of that fact. Being a Christian meant you were willing to give up everything to belong to one whom you had never seen. Being a Christian meant that you were separated from the world to be sanctified, or set apart, for Christ's use. Being a Christian meant that you had become Christ's slave. It meant that you belonged to a strange society called the church. To the philosophers of the age, this was ridiculous. To the powers of the age, this was condemnable. It was treason. Being a Christian meant that you gave your allegiance to a King who was no longer seen by the eyes of the earth, but only by the eyes of the faith. This is why it was so dramatic that King Agrippa would say to Paul, "You almost persuade me to become a Christian." (Acts 26:28) Agrippa was not saying, "Paul, you almost persuaded me to accept Jesus Christ as my personal savior." No, instead Agrippa was saying, "Paul, you almost persuade me to acknowledge that Jesus Christ, risen from the dead, is King of the Jews. Paul, you almost persuade me to join your cause." Agrippa knew the arguments. Agrippa saw the evidence. But Agrippa was not willing to give up everything he was accustomed to having that would have gotten in the way of joining the side of Christ.

Contrary to the notion that becoming a Christian means accepting Christ as your savior, becoming a Christian instead means something much more objective. It is like putting on a new suit. Being a Christian is something you wear. It affects the way you talk, the way you spend your time, the way you look, even the way you eat. It means converting from a life that is *against* Christ to a life that is *for* Christ, like switching sides in a battle. In fact, being a Christian has more to do with what you are a part of than any awakening that has happened inside of you. Being a Christian means that your life has been marked by three things in particular, and each of these three things must be in place in order for you to be called a Christian.

First, you must belong to the faith. That is, you must hold to the essential doctrines of Christian teaching, namely the ecumenical doctrines found in the Apostle's Creed. Notice I did not say that you must have faith. *Having* faith and belonging to *the* faith are two different matters. *The* faith is a system of belief. It is the faith of Christ himself. It is the teachings of the Bible. To be rightfully called a Christian, you must acknowledge and believe that the essential doctrines of the Scriptures are true and good.

Secondly, you must validate your confession by your life. You must live for Christ. This means that you must repent of you sins, use the means that God has given you for spiritual growth, and make an earnest effort to live as Christ's disciple. To rightfully be called a Christian, you must follow Christ.

Finally, and in accordance with our broader topic at hand, you must be baptized. You must be set apart by God for the life of a Christian. You must bear the sign of Christianity. You must go public in the faith. If you have been living under a different system of belief, you must be converted.

These three things are essential in order to be called a Christian. If you are baptized and live a good life but you believe in three Gods instead of one or you deny the virgin birth, then you are not a Christian. If you are baptized and confess the true faith but despise the Word of God in your life by practicing unrepentant rebellion, then you are not a Christian. Furthermore, if you confess the true faith and live a godly life but are not baptized, then you not a Christian. A Christian is one who has been made a disciple by God. Baptism is God's means of making disciples. We will discuss this further later on, but the point I wish to make here before continuing on with the nature of baptism is that baptism, like being called a Christian, is an objective label. It is not dependent upon our personal testimony. It is dependent upon the testimony of others outside of ourselves, especially the testimony of God himself in the person and work of Jesus Christ. Baptism is not only a sacrament, but a sacrament of the church. The church is an objective, visible, tangible entity of the kingdom of Christ. The church, as it is Christ's body, is never a personal or internal matter.

This is not to say that Christianity lacks experiential or subjective elements. There is a great deal of subjectivity in knowing and following Christ. Yet in the matter of being called a Christian, there is little or none in the area of subjectivity. It is completely measureable by others according to the standards given to us by God. The term 'Christian' simply means 'of Christ' or 'belonging to Christ'. This is why we can speak of Christian nations, or Christian music, or Christian art, or Christian businesses. It is not as though the nation or the song or the painting or the business will die and go to Heaven, but rather that those things, in the function of which they were intended, have been expressly set aside for the glory of Christ. The nation purposes to establish Christ-honoring standards of justice. The song purposes to express Christ-honoring music and lyrics. The painting purposes to depict a subject in a Christ-honoring way. The business purposes to conduct itself with Christ-honoring ethics and economics. We may call these entities 'Christian' because they are created or operated by Christian people in a Christian way. In the same manner, a Christian is someone who has been set apart by the Creator, or operator, of his life for the purpose of honoring Christ as a lifestyle. How well they do this is another matter, for we know that Christ will look upon all his Christians on the last day and say to some, "I never knew you; depart from me." (Matt. 7:21-23; 25:31-44) That is why, after all is said and done, there will be a large number of Christians in Hell. Being called a Christian means that you have been enrolled on the winning side. It doesn't mean that you are personally a winner. This may prove to be a mere side note in our discussion of baptism, but it is worth noting because the act of baptism, as we will see, is a confession of faith, a confession quite independent of motive. Baptism does not become baptism only if the recipient really, really means it. Baptism is baptism because God really, really says it is. That is why baptism is also called a christening. It is a naming ceremony. It names us 'Christian'. Internalizing the naming rite is to obscure the matter. It is to tell God that his naming ceremony isn't good enough and that we need more evidence. "But God", we might say, "We need to watch him closely for a while to see if your Spirit is really at work." No, God handles things differently. God has already shown he is at work in the offer of baptism.

6
LAW OR GOSPEL?

Is baptism law? Or is it gospel? Is baptism something that we do for God or something that God does for us? Is baptism an issue of morality, or is it a matter of good news? Are we baptized in order to give something? Or is it to receive something? Do we submit ourselves to the waters of baptism because Christ is the 'only lawgiver'? Or is it because Christ is the only hope of salvation? The answers to these questions are critical to our understanding of the nature of baptism and, consequently, to its uses.

I suppose someone might call this a false dichotomy. I suppose someone might answer and say that baptism is both. I suppose that would be a fine answer and no doubt true in a sense. We cannot deny that baptism was given by Christ as a command and therefore, in that sense, is a law. Nor can we deny that baptism has certain benefits for the recipient and therefore can rightly be called grace. Therefore, obedience is given and benefits are received. But that answer is insufficient. Just because a thing is grace does not make it gospel, and just because a thing is a command does not make it law in the strict sense. God's law is a gracious gift to his people, granted, but that does not mean it frees us from our sins. In fact, it does the opposite. It increases our sins. Furthermore, every command is not law in the same way that we are commanded to honor our parents. For instance, we are commanded to humble ourselves. This does not mean that 'humbling ourselves' should be placed upon the same shelf as 'not stealing'. Calling baptism a gracious law says nothing as to the real purpose of baptism.

Where, then, does its significance lie? Does it function as a law, or does it function as the gospel? Is it a moral injunction, or is it good news? Saying that the answer is both is just as trite as saying that the answer is neither because to open both floodgates is to dilute the question with murky waters and blur the distinction between law and gospel. Consequently, the nature of baptism will not be seen as clearly as it should.

Baptism is a command, but it is a gospel command. It has no business sitting upon the same shelf as the law. It is not a moral issue. Ignoring baptism is certainly a sin, but not because it offends God's holiness. Ignoring baptism is a sin because it offends God's grace. It has its right place in our systematics. It sits right there in the section on the church. But the problem occurs when we use it. We take it off the proper shelf and forget to put it back. It ends up getting placed on the law shelf – not usually with things like murder and stealing – but with incidentals, things like praying before meals and witnessing to my neighbor, things that are good and right, things that we agree we should do, but things without the same moral weight as, for instance, adultery. And if there are any who do equate the neglect of baptism with committing adultery on the basis of Christ being the 'only lawgiver', then we have a whole other problem altogether.

The reality is that baptism is something that God does – not us. It was God who parted the Red Sea for the fleeing Israelites. Sure, Moses had to lift up his rod in obedience. Sure, the people had to obey by traveling through a precarious situation. But who in their right mind would give the credit for the escape to Moses's magical stick or the Israelites' fast running shoes? It is God who saved them. It is God who told them to go forward. It is God who told Moses to lift his rod. Then it was God who came between the Israelite camp and the camp of the Egyptians to become "darkness to the one and light to the other." (Ex. 14.20) It was God who baptized the Israelites in the wilderness, for in the words of the Apostle Paul,

"All were baptized into Moses in the cloud and in the sea." (1 Cor. 10:2) Yes, the parting of the Red Sea was a baptism. It was a covenant of water. Just as Abraham parted the animals by cutting the animals in two, setting the pieces opposite each other, and watched as God passed between them as a testimony to a covenant promise, (Gen. 15:17-18) just as God brought the animals upon the ark of Noah two by two before shutting them up in safety, (Gen. 8:15-16) so too was the parting of the Red Sea a testimony of God's love and faithfulness to the promises he made to his chosen ones. The Red Sea was a baptism to be sure, but it was frightening. It was frightening and dangerous. It was full of love and hate, deliverance and destruction, salvation and condemnation. Yes, the Egyptians were baptized as well. In fact, they were immersed. And it was their judgment. In fact, if I am thinking straight, it seems to me that both of the major examples of baptism by immersion in the Scriptures are examples of judgment, the other obviously being the Great Flood. But for the Israelites, passing though the waters was their salvation. It was the work of a covenant keeping God. It was the gospel. That is why "The people feared the Lord, and believed the Lord and his servant Moses." (Ex. 14:31) The Israelites experienced firsthand the salvation of the Lord expressed in the waters of the Red Sea. It was deliverance in a tangible way. The Israelites saw the dead Egyptian bodies lying on the seashore. They saw the waters parting and then crashing down again. God still saves people tangibly. God still gives us saving signs – not so that we put our trust in the signs – but so that we put our trust in God who saves us *through* the signs.

    This is the beauty and mystery of baptism. God does this wonderful thing. He takes pity on mankind. He has compassion upon sinners. He looks upon those who have offended him and he sets his love upon them. He collides with mankind in the incarnation. He keeps his own covenant in man's place. He suffers for man. He dies for man. He forsakes himself. He rises up from death. He conquers death. He binds the devil. He distributes and proclaims this truth throughout the world. And many come to believe it. And many who come to believe it begin to doubt it. Many forget about it. Many cannot comprehend it. Many are perplexed by it. After all, we can't see it. Then we begin to wonder: what if all those great deeds were not for me? How can I be sure God really loves me? How do I know that I am among the elect? Maybe I don't actually have the faith that I think I have. How can I be sure I believe? How do I know it's all true?

When we speak of salvation by faith, we don't really mean salvation *by faith*. What we mean is salvation by Christ. It is Christ who saves us by making atonement for our sins in his sacrificial death, and not only so, but by coming alive again. Faith is not the foundation upon which our salvation rests. Faith is only a means, an instrument so to speak, that God uses in bringing us to himself. It unites us to Christ. In so doing, the blood of Christ, the true symbol of atonement, is applied to the sinner, just as it is written: "...Christ Jesus, whom God has set forth as a propitiation by His blood, through faith, to demonstrate His righteousness..." (Rom. 3:25) It is faith which makes Christ's atonement *our* atonement. The death of Christ was a demonstration of his righteousness every bit as much as it was a demonstration of his love. But we still have to bridge that gap between the atonement being a demonstration and it being our salvation. Christ's death makes an objective statement about God and about the world, but the doubter might ask, "What does that all have to do with me?"

Baptism holds the answer when our faith fails to grasp it. Our faith is totally insufficient for saving us. It is incapable of keeping us in Christ. It is the Holy Spirit who holds onto *us*, not the other way around. Baptism is God's means of doing that. It is our assurance that the atonement of Christ, the shedding of his blood, was really for *us*, because the water was applied to us and we were washed clean. By knowing this, by remembering this tangible grace, by seeing the water flowing, dripping, cleansing, whether upon ourselves or witnessing it upon another and knowing that this was done to us as well, we are strengthened in our assurance of our belonging to Christ. That is why the writer of Hebrews can say, "Therefore, brethren, having boldness to enter the Holiest by the blood of Jesus, by a new and living way which He consecrated for us, through the veil, that is, His flesh, and having a High Priest over the house of God, let us draw near with a true heart in full assurance of faith, having our hearts sprinkled from an evil conscience and our bodies washed with pure water." (Heb. 10:19-22)

Jesus, the High priest, performs our baptism ceremony. He sprinkles our hearts from an evil conscience and he washes our bodies with pure water. Christ has earned the right to do that for his people. Just as he washed his disciples feet, even against their protests, so Christ baptizes those he calls into his kingdom. Was Christ's washing of his disciples' feet law or gospel? Anytime Christ washes sinners it is gospel. To be washed by God is always gospel. And it is in this washing, this ceremonial cleansing which is described in the tenth chapter of Hebrews, that we are invited to "draw near with a true heart in full assurance of faith." It is in the washing of our bodies in the sacrament of baptism that we can be certain that God loves us and gave his Son as an atoning sacrifice for our sins.

Baptism is so much more than a public proclamation of our personal faith. Baptism is so much more than following Christ in obedience. It is so much more than an outward sign of a previous inward experience. It is the very work of God himself in sanctifying a people for his own pleasure. It is part of his work of salvation. It is part of his calling us out of the darkness and into his wonderful light. It is the seal of the promises of redemption. It is a means of grace. It is a means of assurance that we belong to God. It strengthens our faith. It sanctifies us. It is gospel through and through. That is why Christ said, "Whoever believes and is baptized will be saved." (Mark 16:16) That is why Ananias had the confidence to tell Paul, "Arise and be baptized, and wash your sins away, calling on the name of the Lord." (Acts 22:16) Baptism cannot be divorced from the gospel. It is just as much a part of God's work as faith and repentance – in fact, even more so – for faith and repentance have a problem that continues to get in the way of my holiness – me! My sin taints my faith and repentance to the point where it may even become unrecognizable. But the waters of baptism have no such problem. It is pure water. It testifies perfectly to the grace of God.

We seem to have gotten it all backwards. Again, faith does not *do* anything. Consequently, faith is the real sign. Faith is simply saying 'Yes' to everything God has said and done. Faith is saying 'Yes, I acknowledge that.' Faith is saying 'Amen!' But faith does not do a thing. It is everything else which does something. It is the preached word that does something. It is Providence that does something. It is Christ's blood that does something. It is the water. It is the wine. It is the bread. It is all of these things. But it is not faith. Faith is just there taking it all in. Faith, in actuality, is *not* doing something. It is *not* running away. It is *not* complaining. It is *not* denying. It is *not* turning a deaf ear. Faith is belief. If it comes down to faith and baptism, give me baptism. Give me something undefiled. Give me strength. My faith is far too weak. My faith needs baptism the way a newborn needs a breast. Just attach me to the one who supplies all my needs. Just let me drink of the life that is provided. Just "Let the water and the blood, from thy riven side which flowed, be of sin the double cure, cleanse me from its guilt and power."[1]

The problem with the baptistic mindset is that the Baptist treats baptism as if it is part of the law rather than the gospel. The baptistic mindset considers obedience to the ordinance as the primary objective. It considers the faith of the recipient to be of greater significance than the cleansing. It considers individual faith to be more important than covenant faith. These considerations are foreign to the Scriptural teachings on baptism. In every instance, baptism is connected in some form or another with the gospel. It is always linked with God's work of grace. Unfortunately, there are those, even on both sides of the discussion, who do not regard baptism as an essential issue. There are those, who for the sake of unity, will agree to disagree. There are those who would prefer to discuss matters, they say, which are closer to the heart of the gospel – matters like justification, regeneration, or even election. But baptism is an essential issue. It speaks to all of those things. There will never be unity if we agree to disagree. Baptism is a matter of gospel. Baptism kisses the gospel – and not just by some little peck on the cheek. It is an intimate, passionate, lip-lock.

7
ELECTION

Election means being appointed, or chosen, to a certain position. At the risk of insulting your intelligence, the concept of election has nothing to do with votes as we have become so accustomed to assuming. When a president is elected to office, he is appointed to that particular post. Votes may help in determining the election, but the election is the appointing, not the voting.

I am sure that most of you reading this are quite aware of the distinction between voting and electing. Furthermore, I am sure the concept of election is well established in your own mind. I only mention this because when it comes to that troublesome little science called theology, the definition of election can sometimes get a little fuzzy.

God elects things. People mainly. But really everything. If it happens, then God has elected it. We usually call this predestination of foreordination. When considering our relationship with God, when meditating upon the amazing fact that he has called us out of the darkness and into his wonderful light, we cannot consider very deeply nor meditate very long before we are confronted with this concept of election. How does a sinner turn to God? Well, of course, the same way you fit a large square peg through a small round hole. You don't.

But we know from experience that sinners do turn to God. We also know from experience – or at least we should – that sinners are sorely unworthy of such an adventure. But they do it anyhow. Somehow, some way, large square pegs are forced through small round holes. This is grace. The origin of this sort of grace is called election.

God doesn't wait for our vote to be cast in his favor. If he did, he would be waiting for as long as it takes Darwin's fish to become a badger. He would be waiting throughout eternity. Our vote would never come. Our salvation is not accomplished by democracy. God chooses. God appoints us. And no, he has not appointed everyone. But the Scriptures are clear. Our redemption is God's work from first to last. (Heb. 12.2) It is God who loves us before we will ever love him. (1 John 4.19) It is God who calls on us before we will ever call upon him. (John 15.16) It is God who makes us alive when we were desperately dead. (Eph. 2.5) It is all God, and it is forever secured for us in the shed blood of Christ.

Look. Look and see how closely linked baptism is to election.

Before I understood that it was God who chose me and not I him, baptism to me was exactly what the baptistic folks purport it to be – inessential, man-centered, and law based. But once election was revealed to me by way of Scripture, baptism naturally took a turn. In fact, for me it was two things. It was the grace found in the water, and it was election. In the grace found in the water I discovered that baptism was gospel. In election I discovered that baptism belongs exclusively to God. I will not try and pretend that it is this way for everyone because it is not. The road to a more biblical understanding of baptism will be different for different people. But for me it was this way. And the concept of election, no matter how less compelling it might be for someone else than it was for me, is still so intricately linked to the topic of baptism that it would be improper to ignore it.

The covenantal nature of faith struck me – the fact that faith is not conjured up inside of myself by innate power, but that it is a gift, that it originates from somewhere outside of myself, from the very heart of God, for we are told that this faith through which we have been saved is "not of yourselves; it is the gift of God, not of works, lest anyone should boast." (Eph. 2.8-9) Faith belongs to God. It is his faith. We only share in it. In fact, it is the faith of Christ in which we share. It is never our own. We may talk about this individual faith, we may call it personal faith, we may try and tout it as something unique to ourselves, we may compare it to that of others, we may call it weak or strong, and sometimes it is appropriate, but if we mean by those terms that the faith which we experience is in some way peculiar to us, that it is actually *ours*, then we have missed the bus completely. Faith is not ours. It is Christ's. He gives it to us by the Holy Spirit.

But furthermore, not only is this faith given to us by God, but we are called his "workmanship". We are crafted by God himself through Christ's faith. We are clay before the potter. "For we are His workmanship, created in Christ Jesus for good works, which God prepared beforehand that we should walk in them." (Eph. 2.10) This is what is meant by the sovereignty of God in salvation. This is election played out upon the stage. This is God choosing – not me choosing. This is "the faith". Yes, it is a faith which originates outside of myself, but a faith of which I am allowed – no, not only allowed, but called – to partake. The Apostle even refers to it elsewhere as *the* faith, as something that can be continued in, grounded in. (1) That is why the Apostle is careful to note those two little words that ring so loudly and so often throughout the New Testament Scriptures – "in Christ".

Everything that we do, everything which we enjoy, everything that we are as part of "the faith" is done, or enjoyed "in Christ". "Just as He chose us *in Him* before the foundation of the world, that we should be holy and without blame before Him in love." (Eph. 1.4)

Who exactly is God's elect? Before you start looking around the sanctuary wondering, consider this: it's easy. Jesus Christ is God's elect. That is what the term Christ means, after all. God's chosen. God's appointed. God's Messiah. Christ is the Seed that was promised to Abraham so that Abraham would become the father of many nations. When the Scriptures mention election, it is always in the context of being in Christ, for it is Christ who was chosen for this impossible task of redemption. We must understand our election – that is, our being chosen – only as it occurs *in Christ*. It is election only so far as there is union. Where there is no union, there is no election. Where there is no election, there is no being 'in Christ'. Therefore, all genuine faith originates and shares in *Christ's* faithfulness, not ours.

Once I understood this, once I recognized that *my* faith, the faith which *I* possessed was really not mine at all but belonged to God 'in Christ'; once I understood this, I read another passage of Scripture in a whole new light. I read that there is only *one* body and *one* Spirit. I read that there is only *one* hope of my calling. Furthermore, there is only *one* Lord, *one* faith, *one* baptism, and *one* God and Father who is above all, through all, and in us all. (Eph. 4.4-6) No wonder, I thought. No wonder my faith is not my own. It is because there is only *one* faith. After all, there is only one God, one Lord, and one Holy Spirit. Faith is a faith that is shared. It is shared *in Christ*. And not only that, but there is only *one* baptism. I realized then that there is no such thing as a personal testimony. There is no such thing as a personal covenant between me and God. God does not make covenant with me. Who am I? My faith is not even my own! God's covenant is with Abraham. Yes, God's covenant is with Abraham and is grounded and secured in Christ. I am only a beneficiary in so far as I am united to Christ. That is why I am called a child of Abraham – if I share in the faith of Abraham. I have no relationship with God whatsoever apart from God's relationship with Abraham, and certainly not apart from the faithfulness of Jesus Christ. There is *one* Lord, *one* faith, *one* baptism.

One baptism. That means that when I am baptized, it is the same baptism as when you are baptized. It means we are both being baptized into the same Lord, into the same faith. It means that when a baby is baptized, it is the same baptism as when a college professor or a state official is baptized. They are both baptized into the same Lord, into the same faith. What it means is that there is not a single baptism that testifies to the faith of the individual recipient. It is not an ordinance which points to the parts. Instead, every baptism testifies to the faith of the whole. In this instance, God is a collectivist. Baptism is about inclusion, not seclusion. After all, "For by one Spirit we were all baptized into one body." (1 Cor. 12.13)

This was my journey. Yours may not be exactly the same. But regardless, understanding the covenantal, unifying, creedal nature of faith is critical in a proper understanding of baptism. Election is expressed in two facets. First, there is the eternal decree of God that is a mystery and will remain a mystery as long as we remain in this body. That is the election which says, "He chose us in Him before the foundations of the world." But there is another train on the track. It is a train we can actually see. Jesus called it the church. Paul calls it Christ's body. It is the communion of saints. It is the company of the elect.

Yes. The elect. The flesh and blood elect. Now it is appropriate to begin looking around the sanctuary. You can find them to your left or to your right. They are there in the pew next to you. They are chewing the same bread as you, sipping the same wine. They are the voice next to you, singing, praying, amening. You don't know their heart. You don't know if they have gotten right with God. They say they have, but how do you really know? They seem decent enough, but do you really know what motivates them, what stirs them deep inside? Who are they? They call themselves Christians, but who are they really?

They are the elect. If they have received baptism, they are the elect. Remember, we don't know the mind of God. God has not set a halo atop the head of those destined for salvation. But he has given us baptism. That is how we know. The secret things belong to God. We don't ride that train. The train we ride is of a different sort. It allows us to see all around us, but only all around us, never above us, and we must be content with that. It is not our place to go around poking and prodding, digging and wrenching, cutting and scraping until the flesh is pulled back away from the Christian soul just enough so that we can sneak a quick peek inside to find evidence to the contrary. Christians must be believers. Not just in God, but in each other. That is why over and over again the writers of the New Testament call the people in the congregation the elect. It is an assumption. Just as baptism is an assumption. Just as the baptistic ideal of baptism is an assumption, all baptism is an assumption. We are assuming that the recipient of the baptism has a right to the baptism. If they have no right, they have no baptism. But the difference between the baptistic crowd and the sacramental crowd is that the Baptist baptizes on the sole basis of human profession. The sacramentalist baptizes on the sole basis of covenant promise. Just as B.B. Warfield once wrote, "Human Profession is no more solid basis to build upon than a Divine promise."[2]

The train we ride is the church train. We ride it together. If we say we are Christians, believe us. If we have been baptized, if we repent of sin, if we confess the true faith and say that we are Christians, believe us. We are. Maybe all of us won't stand up on the final day. Maybe some will fail the test. But for now, aboard the church train, believe us. That is the facet of election that the Scriptures refer to more often than not. Baptism is our calling. Baptism is the work of the Holy Spirit. Baptism is election as it rubs elbows with us every day.

PART TWO

WHAT DOES BAPTISM DO?

8

MAKING CHRISTIANS

We've explored what baptism is. A cleansing ritual. A sacrament. Gospel. Election on an earthly scale. Let's move forward to what baptism does, and because it is a sacrament, it must at least accomplish *something*. It does. In fact it accomplishes more than one thing. It accomplishes a number of things, the first of which I have made mention of already a couple of times, and because of that, I will attempt not to linger too long upon this point. The first thing baptism does is make Christians. It is conversion.

Baptism takes somebody who is naturally outside of the faith and converts them to Christianity. Remember, becoming a Christian is like putting on a new suit. It is something you wear. It is going from the darkness to the light, from the world of the dead to the world of the living. King Clovis [1] went from being a ruthless warrior to becoming a Christian overnight through the rite of baptism, not so that he would stop being ruthless, but to the contrary, so that he could now be ruthless in the name of Christ. But what baptism failed to restrain in Clovis, it worked mightily in the kingdom of the Franks, because in the conversion of Clovis so came the conversion of a nation, the name of Christ being exalted while the pagan practices were trampled underfoot. When Clovis took his wife's God as his own, the world literally changed.

In this sense, baptism is identification, or as I mentioned previously, a naming rite. It is the act of becoming identified with Christ when by nature we are identified with the world. It is the act of being pronounced 'Christian'. It is the putting away of the old name and the putting on of the new. Our parents named us one thing in accordance with their will, identifying us with whatever connotations our name carries. Christ names us after himself. Christ is in the business of renaming fallen man. He is in the business of enlisting recruits. He is in the business of gathering followers. He does it by dousing them with water in his own name. This is his mark upon us. He brands us. He owns us. We are his. No longer do we wander about in search of an identity. We have one. We are Christians. We are 'in Christ'.

    Christ wants more disciples. It is for this purpose that he sent the twelve to the ends of the earth. It is for this purpose that he continues to send his people forth, even to this very day. And how are disciples made? By sharing our own testimonies? By stirring up emotions? By appealing to felt needs? By inducing a certain kind of prayer? Certainly not! It is by baptism. That is what our Lord taught us. He instructed his apostles upon his ascension to go into the world and make disciples by baptizing. Baptizing and teaching. Yes, teaching is vital, but it is no more vital than baptism. Baptism is no less important than teaching. They are on equal terms. "Go therefore, and make disciples of all the nations," said the Lord, "Baptizing them in the name of the Father and of the Son and of the Holy Spirit, teaching them to observe all the things that I have commanded you." (Matt. 28:18-20) There it is. Baptism and teaching. Together, making disciples. Where there is no baptism, there is no disciple. Where there is no teaching, there is no disciple. Remember the three marks of a Christian: right belief, right practice, and right baptism.

    Let us be careful not to insist that making disciples is something different than baptizing them. Let us be careful not to insist that what Jesus really meant was that we make disciples first and then baptize them second as if baptism is a subordinate aspect of the disciple-making process. "But," one might ask, "Isn't instruction basic to discipleship? For how can a disciple be made without being taught?" Yes, that is true, instruction certainly is fundamental in the disciple making process. But Jesus put baptism and instruction on the same plain. He said make disciples. Then he said baptize them and teach them. Therefore, baptism is just as basic to discipleship as instruction. Jesus touts baptism and instruction in the same breath. In other words, you make disciples by baptizing them and teaching them to follow Christ. We must not reverse this, nor may we take the teaching and discard the baptism altogether. To do so is to devalue the words of Christ. To do so is to set ourselves up as judges over Christ. We must not take his words to mean that once someone believes we make disciples by teaching them about Christ and then baptizing them sometime later. That is a perversion of Christ's words, plain and simple. Rather, once someone believes, the proper thing to do is baptize them and teach them. That is called making disciples.

Just to be clear, baptism and instruction go hand in hand. If we go about baptizing everyone we see and leaving them to return to the gutter where we found them, then we will have a lot of wet gutter dwellers, and they will dry quickly, and they will go on living in the gutter. Baptism must be accompanied by the Word. It is the Word that gives life. That is why Luther said "For without God's word the water is plain water and no baptism. But with the word of God it is a baptism, that is, a life-giving water…"(2) But at the same time, baptism should never be neglected at the expense of instruction. Instruction must have a context. It must have a place to live. If we go about instructing gutter dwellers about what life is like outside the gutter but never offer them a place in our churches, then we have wasted a lot of breath and valuable time, for they will soon find out that it is quite difficult to live a life of Heaven when no one has bothered to bring you out of the gutter. The Word must be taught in the context of baptism. It is baptism that makes us Christians. It is baptism that admits us into the fellowship of the church. It is baptism that engrafts us into the body of Christ. It is the Word of God that ensures that our baptism does not return to us void.

If you are discipling your child and you are doing so apart from baptism, then you are discipling in a vacuum. If you are washing your children in the Word but have not brought them forth to be washed by the waters of baptism, then you are not getting them fully clean. Baptism is essential to discipleship in a similar way that sticking a flag in the ground is essential to conquering a nation. It is a reference point. It is a lasting sign lest we forget whose land we're living on. And we forget far too easily.

9
SIGNS AND SEALS

First of all, we are told that "Abraham believed God, and it was accounted to him for righteousness". (Rom.4.3) In other words, it was faith which brought the righteousness of God to bear upon the life of Abraham. It was faith by which God set him straight. You see, Abraham was crooked. He needed a great deal of straightening. He was all out of sorts. He needed a whole lot of getting put back together. In the eyes of God, like each of us, Abraham was a mess. But in the eyes of God, Abraham was made right. He was cleaned up. He was justified because he was justifiable. All it took was for him to believe something which was told to him. All it took was God telling him something unbelievable. God was a complete stranger who would become an intimate friend. All Abraham had to do was listen. Listen and take it all in. Listen and take it all in and act upon it.

However, despite his gigantic faith, righteousness still had nothing to do with Abraham. It had everything to do with God. It took an upright God to straighten out a crooked Abraham. All Abraham had to do was say, "Yes Lord," and it was done. It was done by God. Righteousness is something which belongs only to God. Justification is something which only God has the power to accomplish. Yet here was this little man, this little lost man with a barren wife and a bleak future who heard God speak. He heard God tell him, "Go!" and he went. He heard God tell him "Look up!" and he looked and saw countless stars. He did not roll his eyes when God told him that his elderly wife would soon birth a child. The land. The inheritance. It was all too much for a simple man like Abraham to believe, but he believed nonetheless. God established his righteousness by way of promise. It was the reception of this promise that qualified Abraham for a life of intimacy with God. God makes it his business to establish his righteousness in the justification of sinners.

But secondly, in addition to being told that Abraham was justified on account of his taking it all in, we are furthermore told that Abraham received of God "the sign of circumcision, a seal of the righteousness of the faith which he had while still uncircumcised." (Rom. 4:11) God is not nice. If there is any proof that God is not nice, then this is it. But God is holy, and he demonstrated his holiness to Abraham by requiring him to undergo a brief but painful and bloody surgical procedure. This was to impress upon Abraham a number of things among which is the fact that covenanting with God is bloody business. But it was the cutting that was significant, the cutting and the peeling back. It was as if God was telling Abraham: 'If you are to belong to me, and if I am going to fix everything that is wrong with you, then you must bear this mark. This mark is painful, but it will heal. This mark will make you different, but I am different. This mark is not only a sign that you are mine but also a sign of how bad of shape you were in before I found you and the price that must be paid to make you right. Oh, and by the way, if you refuse the sign, if you refuse to cut yourself, then I will take matters into my own hands, but it won't be a circumcision. It will be a complete severing from the body. And one final thing. It is not only for you, but for your posterity, for every male born or bought, for my covenant is for you and those that come after you.' (Gen. Ch. 17)

Do you think Abraham considered the cost? Did he engage in a cost/benefit analysis? Did he really think for a minute that the circumcision of a ninety-nine year old man was not worth the exchange of an entire kingdom? That is what he was promised, after all – a kingdom. He was going to become the father of many nations. He was to become the father of the Gentiles. This little lost man was to inherit the earth, all because a holy God decided to set him straight in righteousness. No, Abraham did not think it too high a price to pay. We are told that Abraham did not waver in unbelief. He received what he was told and acted upon it like an obedient child who was always ready to answer "Yes sir" or "Yes ma'am." No wonder Isaac laid himself upon the alter so submissively. He learned it from his father. Fathers, if we desire obedient children, we must learn to be submissive ourselves. Notice the trust that existed between father and son. Notice how in the life of Abraham, faith and obedience were common bedfellows.

So we are told that circumcision was a sign. It was a sign of the covenant that God made with Abraham. It was a sign of the promises. It was a sign of the obligations. It was a sign of the need for redemption. It was a sign of salvation itself. It was a sign of the gospel. But it was not only a sign. We are told that it was also a seal. It was a "seal of the righteousness of the faith which he had while still uncircumcised." A seal of the righteousness of the faith. Whatever does that mean?

The fact that circumcision acted as a seal means that it was more than a sign. It was the bond in the covenant. The sign was there to act as an object lesson. The seal was there to act like glue. It holds the model airplane together. God initiates a covenant grounded in a real, divine promise, and he sets up a sign as a memorial unto that promise, but the memorial is more than a sign – it does more than showcase the promise – it confirms the promise; it bears witness to the surety of the promise. In other words, the covenant seal is a testimony to the authenticity and reliability of the covenant maker.

So when we are told that Abraham's circumcision was "a seal of the righteousness of the faith which he had while still uncircumcised", we are being told that his circumcision was to be unto him a token of a divine promise, of something great which was waiting for him, of a certain and without-a-doubt very real reward within his grasp. The sign helped him believe. He carried it around with him everywhere he went. And because he bore the sign upon his own body, he could be certain that he had been sealed unto the Lord his God. He had been sanctified, and there was nothing – no powers, no passions, no other purpose upon this earth – that could tear that seal apart. He belonged to God and his circumcision was proof.

But please don't misunderstand. He was not considered righteous by virtue of the circumcision. That is the whole point of the emphasis on his being righteous *before* the cutting took place. The circumcision was given as a seal of the righteousness that came by virtue of a divine promise. The covenant sign did not work as an ipso facto blessing. It was not an ATM for salvation. It is not considered grace because it was sufficient for Abraham's salvation; rather, it is grace because it bears witness to the God who saves, and not only that, but to the reliability of the promise of the God who saves. The righteousness was a gift of God. The circumcision was the sign and the seal of that righteousness. That is why it was just as effective for Abraham *after* he was called righteous as it was for his son Isaac *before* he was even old enough to smile. The righteousness of God transcends our faith in him. That is why the covenant sign is not necessarily tied to the moment of the thing which it signifies. That is why it is just as valid before one is justified as after. The covenant sign is a sign of God's righteousness rather than a sign of our faith.

This, I am afraid, is one of the grave errors of baptistic thinking. The Baptist insists that faith must be present for the sign to be received. This thinking implies that the sign points to personal faith. This is not how it was for Abraham. The sign pointed not to his faith but to the righteousness of God. Faith need not be present in the recipient of the sign for the sign to be valid. Faith only needs to be present in the administration of the sign, which is, in fact, the very nature of the sign. The sign is, in itself, in some measure, whether great or small, an act of faith. It is saying that the individual who is receiving this sign has a right to receive it, not because of any righteousness in him, but rather because he belongs to God and God is faithful in his righteousness.

But this is circumcision. What does circumcision have to do with baptism? Well, nothing and everything. Nothing in the sense that baptism is not the same procedure as circumcision, but everything in the sense that baptism is not an entirely different procedure than circumcision. What circumcision signified in the cutting and bleeding of the flesh baptism signifies in its washing and cleansing. Both are signs of a covenant. One is dead while the other is alive. Both are signs of the gospel. One uses blood while the other uses water. Both are signs of God's righteousness. One is for males only while the other includes females. We could go on and on about this but the importance lies here: that the apostle Paul not only says that we still need circumcision, but he calls the procedure by the name of baptism. He says we have been "circumcised by the circumcision made without hands...by the circumcision of Christ, buried with him in baptism..." (Col. 2.11) Paul says we still need to be circumcised, but that we don't go around cutting people anymore so that they can bear God's mark. Instead, we baptize them. The application of water is a circumcision far better than the cutting of the foreskin because baptism is a circumcision done by Christ. Baptism replaces circumcision in God's covenant economy. In other words, the old ritual is dead in practice. The new ritual is alive in Christ. This is demonstrated in the Savior's own baptism. Christ, by his baptism, was not saying that he needs the gospel. Rather, he was saying that he *is* the gospel. To be baptized into the name of Christ is gospel from first to last. It is the revelation of Christ in our lives. That is why the Apostle goes on to mention that in baptism, in the circumcision which is done by Christ, that "you, being dead in your trespasses and the uncircumcision of your flesh, He has made alive together with Him, having forgiven you all trespasses." (Col. 2:13)

Can you see how baptism provides assurance of salvation? It is not because baptism is sufficient to this end, nor is it because there exists some mystical power in the water. Baptism provides assurance because it is not only a sign of what God has done, but it actually applies what he has done to us directly so that we might have faith. It is not a sign of our faith – no, on the contrary – it is a place for faith to live. It is a home. It is a mother. It is a spring from which faith may bubble up. It is where faith is nurtured and the Holy Spirit is hard at work. Baptism is the water that helps the flower to grow. Baptism can be rejected, no doubt. But to reject it is to reject the work of God in your life. To reject it is to say 'No' to the one thing that gave that little lost man Abraham a sure and glorious future; it is to say 'No' to the promise of God which says "I will be your God and you will be my people." (Ex. 6:7) Who wants to say no to that?

10
UNION WITH CHRIST

Allow me to ask a controversial question. Can an unbeliever have communion with Christ? Can someone who is still dead in sins be united to Jesus? Is it possible? No, you say? Well, that makes sense. It seems inconceivable, doesn't it? After all, "What fellowship has righteousness with lawlessness? And what communion has light with darkness?" (2 Cor. 6:14)

There is a difference, however, between pagans and hypocrites. Pagans sin ignorantly. Hypocrites know exactly what they are doing. Hypocrisy is a problem, no doubt. But, depending upon what we mean by the term, hypocrisy is exactly the kind of problem that the church needs. If what we mean by hypocrisy is pharaseeism, the art of pointing out your neighbor's sleepies when you have a two-by-four jammed into your own retina, then we could do without it. In fact, we would do well to expunge that form of hypocrisy from every dark, dusty corner of our world. But if what we mean by hypocrisy is not being, on the inside, everything we appear to be on the outside, then let's lift our glasses in a toast to human frailty, for this is the struggle of the life that is in Christ. It is not a struggle to conform the outside to what we wish we were on the inside, for that would only be dishonest; neither is it a struggle to conform the inside to the image we present on the outside, for that would only be self-righteous. The struggle is to move forward in this terrible tension. The struggle is to conform both the inside *and* the outside to the life that is to be lived in Christ. The struggle is to improve our union with the Savior.

There is a sense in which a hypocrite may indeed live in communion with Christ despite the fact that light has nothing in common with darkness. You see, hypocrites don't necessarily live in darkness. Pagans live in darkness. Hypocrites live in the light and feed off the darkness. That is what makes hypocrisy so dangerous. That is what makes hypocrisy hypocrisy. The reality of this tension between our sin and the expectation to put on a front is what makes union with Christ like a stick of dynamite – thrilling or destructive depending on its use. This tension has the potential to spark an explosion of passion and reform or turn entire structures into a heap of ash. This tension is not a problem in itself. It can be humbling, as a matter of fact. A humble hypocrite is a good hypocrite. These are the ones who confess that they are not what they should be. They may act better than they really are, but they are not afraid to admit it. The church needs more of these. What the church doesn't need are pretentious players. These are the ones who put on a good show – sometimes theologically; sometimes practically – all the while damaging relationships, sowing discord, and dividing churches. You might call them wolves in sheep's clothing, though they may not always be wolves. They might just be bad sheep. Sometimes they are malicious; sometimes they are just mistaken, but whatever the motive, their behavior cannot be tolerated. With that being said, however, can they still not be saved?

   The aim here is not to analyze every type of Christian. I only want to distinguish between those who are considered faithful and those who will one day be told "I never knew you; depart from Me, you who practice lawlessness!" (Matt. 7.23) The latter are obviously hypocrites in some form. Certainly they must have put on an appearance of godliness. But they were never made right with God. Some would say that it was because they were not elect. But were they not counted among the people? Were they not called out from among the pagans? Did they not taste the heavenly gift? Certainly they were elected in some form, were they not? Others would say that their falling away is proof that they never belonged to Christ in the first place. But did they really fall away? Did they not do great things in Christ's name? Did they not keep the fire burning until the day they died? Still others would say that they had salvation but lost it. But how can this be? How can you lose an eternal gift? How can you not keep something that God has promised to secure?

The first thing we must recognize is that every single Christian – myself, you reading this book, the greatest minister to the lowliest babe – each of us has the potential to be the one to whom Christ speaks those tragic words. Each one of us lives in the danger of becoming the tragic hypocrite. That is the tension of union with Christ. The union is glorious if we abide in it, but deadly if we do not. Regardless, let us not pretend that the union was never there. When Christ says, "I never knew you", is he implying that there was never union? Is he saying that there was never hope to begin with? Was it all a façade? Or could the tragic hypocrite have improved his union? Could he have moved forward in the great tension of his hypocrisy, conforming both inwardly and outwardly to the image of his Savior? Could not the pretentious player have become the humble hypocrite and saved himself from his impending doom? Could he not have just heard the promises and taken them all in and hid them in his heart?

We are all hypocrites in some form. Maybe we talk about the importance of prayer but pray very little ourselves. Maybe we mention a time we shared Christ and make it seem like it is a regular part of our life when it really isn't. Maybe we talk of purity but harbor lusts in our hearts. Maybe we minister to the lost but ignore our own children. Maybe we talk about our love for fellowship but bounce around from church to church. Whatever the reason, we are all hypocrites. Sinners are hypocrites. But let us focus for a moment upon the really bad ones. Let's even call them unregenerate for the sake of argument. Let us call them Christians, but let us call them unbelievers. Will you indulge me that? Do they experience real union with Christ? Two striking examples come to mind. The first is the rock in the wilderness. The second is the metaphor of the vine and the branches.

The Israelites were wandering and thirsty. They were also complaining an awful lot. In fact, we are told that their complaining was due to unbelief. Because of this unbelief, an entire generation was kept from entering the land of promise. Yes, it was a land given by way of a divine promise. Yet this was not an unconditional promise; it had to be received. It had to be believed upon. It had to be taken. But it came by promise nonetheless. The problem was, however, that "with most of them God was not well pleased, for their bodies were scattered in the wilderness." (1 Cor. 10:5) We are told that their destruction is for us an example of faithlessness. If we are faithless, even though we have been included in the covenant of faith, we are living in danger. If we complain, if we commit sexual immorality or idolatries or lust after evil things, if we turn our hearts away from the one who bought us, if we live this way we are in danger of the same fate as the unbelieving Israelites. But there is something extraordinary in this exhortation – something beautiful and frightening. Those who died in the wilderness – despite their unbelief, despite their sin, despite their turning – those whose bodies were scattered were still united to Christ.

We are told that they all ate the same spiritual food and drank the same spiritual drink. (1 Cor. 10:3-4) Even more amazingly, however, we are told that they drank from the same spiritual source. They drank from Christ himself. Yes, it's true! Those that lived and those that died, each to his own person, drew his sustenance from Christ himself. They partook in the Savior. They fellowshipped with the very Son of God through the sacrament of the rock. They were part of him. Though they fell in unbelief, they were every bit part of the body of Christ as those who lived and entered the land of promise.

It doesn't get much more inclusive than this. The damned hypocrites were joined to Christ.

Now don't get me wrong. Just because they were part of the body of Christ does not mean that they currently enjoy eternal life, for "with most of them God was not well pleased." But what it does mean is that it is quite possible to have genuine union with Christ and still be damned. It should be sobering to us to know that apostasy really exists, and that if we fail to take care of the faith entrusted to us then we too might die in the desert. But isn't it also wonderful? Isn't it just beautiful how the gospel invitation extends to each and every covenant member? If Christ does not exclude all hypocrites from his fellowship, then why should we exclude them from ours? To be sure, it is not all hypocrites with whom Christ will break bread. There are certainly those pretentious players with whom he has no affection. But Christ is no respecter of persons. If there are those who draw their sustenance from Christ while hating him in their hearts, they will be cut off, no doubt. But isn't it wonderful to know that the land of promise has already been set before us and that all we have to do is take it? Not only the best of us may take it, but each and every one, from the least to the greatest?

This is exactly Christ's point in his metaphor of the vine and the branches. "I am the true vine, and My Father is the vinedresser. Every branch in Me that does not bear fruit He takes away..." (John 15.1-2) Notice the "in Me." Christ is saying that there are branches, bad branches that are "In Christ." These bad branches have genuine fellowship with the Lord, but they bear no fruit. They are part of the vine, but they are faithless branches. Though they draw their sustenance from Christ, they will be cut off because they fail to produce. They fail to abide in the vine. Yes, being united with Christ comes with a cost. There is a duty. There is an obligation. We must abide in him. This is what Paul means when he admonishes the Christians in Rome by reminding them, "Do not be haughty, but fear. For if God did not spare the natural branches, He may not spare you either." (Rom. 11:19-21) In other words, if God did not bear with national Israel in her unbelief, then why should the Gentiles expect God to continue to sustain them if they also commit the same sins as Israel?

The same concept is true in the metaphor of the lampstands. Christ threatens to cut off the Ephesians if they fail to repent. (Rev. 2:5) Certainly the Ephesians had union with Christ. Certainly they shared in the fellowship of the Savior. But though fellowship with Christ is a safe place in regard to his power to save, fellowship with Christ is a dangerous place for those who are living in sin and refuse to repent. Christ says that he will remove their lampstand. He will snuff them out. He will tear the cancer from the body. Sure, it will leave a wound. It always does when God performs this kind of surgery. But the wound will heal, and the church will be better off because of it.

I say all that to say simply this: that baptism is union with Christ. And it is genuine. And yes, it produces hypocrites. But this is no reason to exclude our children from the waters. We are all hypocrites to some degree. The duty of the church and the family is to produce humble hypocrites rather than pretentious players. The duty of the church and the family is to bear one another's burdens, to help each other along in moving forward in the terrible tension of conforming both the inside and the outside to the image of Christ. Children belong. Children drink from the Rock just as the rest of us do. Sure, some will prove faithless. But adults will prove faithless as well. Again, God is not a respecter of persons. The invitation is there. The land is waiting. Take it. Simple as that. Take it and live.

One more thing. Let's revisit briefly Romans chapter six. Let me set it before you. Read it carefully. See the promise. See the union. See the baptism. See the obligations. See the relationship between them all. See them and believe.

"What shall we say then? Shall we continue in sin so that grace may abound? Certainly not! How shall we who died to sin live any longer in it? Or do you not know that as many of us as were baptized into Christ Jesus were baptized into his death? Therefore we were buried with him through baptism into death, that just as Christ was raised from the dead by the glory of the Father, even so we also should walk in newness of life. For if we have been united together in the likeness of His death, certainly we also shall be in the likeness of His resurrection…"

11
REMISSION OF SINS

The Nicene Creed, adopted at the Council of Nicea in the fourth century, reads "We acknowledge one baptism for the remission of sins." As moderns, what are we to make of that statement? It is, after all, a central doctrine of the historic, Christian church. Are we to brush it off as outdated? Has the church moved passed such archaic teachings? Has our understanding of the purpose of baptism evolved so much in the last sixteen hundred years that we can ignore the plain doctrines of the past? It seems that we have. Who teaches this anymore? With all the talk of reformation and getting back to the gospel, who is teaching that forgiveness is dependent upon baptism? Who is teaching the Nicene Creed?

I do not want to sound over-dramatic, for certainly *some* Christians haven't forgotten. Yet I am also certain that the vast majority of modern Christians have never even heard of the Nicene Creed and most of those who have heard of it have no idea what it says. Is this acceptable? Is it proper to ignore the ancient creeds of the church? Are we justified in this? If so, are we also justified in ignoring the teachings of Holy Scripture as well – Scripture such as "Repent, and let every one of you be baptized in the name of Jesus Christ for the remission of sins…" (Acts 2.38) or "Arise and be baptized, and wash away your sins, calling on the name of the Lord"? (Acts 22.16) Did the early church misunderstand these texts, or have we moderns experienced some sort of glitch in our ability to process historical theology? Does baptism really have this kind of power – the power of forgiveness?

The first thing we must admit, at the very least, is that the Scriptures *appear* to give baptism this kind of power. In some way or another, the Word of God ties baptism to forgiveness. The question is: how tightly is it tied and in what way? We must not gloss over this point. We must not come to these passages and choose not to deal with them. We must not push them aside because they don't fit into our theological paradigm, assuming that they must mean something else instead of what they actually say because certainly they can't possibly mean *that*. Let's not become content with shoving them under our beds or into a corner of the room and throwing a blanket over them and calling our floor clean. God's Word attributes forgiveness to baptism in at least some measure, and if we are to be good disciples we must figure out how.

The first thing we can do is to argue it away. We can rationalize. We can force it into our own box. We can listen to the Apostle Peter's words and we can hear "Repent! Repent for the forgiveness of sins!" We can hear that and we can set the baptism aside. Then, after we are quite sure that the point of "Repent!" has been driven home, we can dust off baptism and in good conscience suggest to our brand new convert that it would be a good idea to get baptized out of obedience to our Lord. That is one way we can read it.

Or perhaps we can pretend that this is a baptism of the Holy Spirit apart from water. We can listen to the Apostle's words and we can hear "Repent! Repent and receive the inward dwelling of the Holy Spirit for the forgiveness of sins! And you shall receive the gift of the Spirit! You, too, may learn new languages!" Then we can tell our brand new convert to go and wait eagerly for this gift as a proof that he has been saved. Then he will wait. And he will wait. And if nothing happens to him he will begin to doubt himself. Then so as not to appear unsaved before his Spirit-filled friends, he will work himself up into a frenzy allowing a few alien sounds to escape from his lips, gaining his assurance from this strange phenomenon.

Or maybe we change the wording a little bit. After all, maybe the word translated 'for' can also be translated 'because'. We can listen to Peter's words and we can hear "Repent! Repent and be baptized *because* of the forgiveness of sins!" Then we can relax now that we have found a reasonable explanation for a text that we could not have otherwise understood. It all makes sense now. We are baptized as a result of our forgiveness of sins! Yet we would be forgetting something. 'Repent' and 'be baptized' are spoken in the same breath. Does that also mean that we are to *repent* because of the forgiveness of sins? Does the forgiveness take place apart from the repentance? Is the repentance, like baptism, an afterthought? Even if it was, it still places baptism on equal terms with repentance and that mystery still remains unresolved.

Or maybe, just maybe, we can read the text for what it says. We can listen to the Apostle Peter's words and we can hear "Repent and be baptized! Repent and be baptized for the forgiveness of sins!" He does not say, "Repent for the forgiveness of your sins and be baptized" as if baptism plays second fiddle to our being forgiven through our repentance; instead, the text is clear that we are to both repent *and* be baptized for the forgiveness of sins. Even if the word was translated 'because' or 'unto' instead of 'for', the message is the same. The repentance *and* the baptism are tied to the forgiveness. In some sense, according to Peter, our being forgiven depends upon our being baptized. It is not "repent *or* be baptized" but "repent *and* be baptized." It is not as though forgiveness is impossible without baptism, but certainly it should not be expected without baptism, for baptism partners with repentance as a means of obtaining forgiveness. Baptism is not subordinate to repentance in importance but only differs in function. Where repentance is the turning to God – the sorrow and resolve of conviction, the plea for deliverance and the bidding farewell to the old ways – baptism is similar yet louder and more visible. It is the counterpart of repentance. It is a sanctifying mark distinguishing you from Christ's enemies. It boldly proclaims that your sins are washed away and that you belong to Christ Jesus. In other words, it is as if the Apostle says, "Turn from your sin unto Christ and be engrafted into his name for the forgiveness of sins!" There is no dichotomy in the present text. We must never drive a wedge between repentance and baptism. They are not precisely the same, but neither are they contrary. We cannot take the one and leave the other in regard to the forgiveness of sins. Peter does not allow it. Repentance and baptism, together, work forgiveness.

Is this not how Paul was to understand the words of Ananias, "Arise and be baptized, and wash away your sins, calling on the name of the Lord"? Is this not what Peter meant in his sermon as well? There is an intimate connection between repenting and being baptized, between calling upon the name of the Lord and washing your sins away. Even so, there is an intimate connection between baptism and the forgiveness of sins. We must at least admit that in some measure our being forgiven depends upon our being baptized.

But what about the thief on the cross? Is it not possible to be forgiven without baptism? Possible, yes. Normative, no. The dying thief was a bit preoccupied at the time; I hope we don't hold that against him. Christ certainly did not. Certainly, the crucified thief is an example to us that baptism is not absolutely necessary for salvation, but then again, is that not the point? It takes an example such as a man nailed to a tree, unable to get down, dying, to teach us that baptism is not absolutely necessary for forgiveness. It takes the extraordinary to keep us from over-emphasizing the ordinary. When the Augsburg Confession declares that baptism is necessary for salvation, it means ordinarily. This is essentially what the Westminster Confession means when it teaches that outside the church "…there is no ordinary possibility of salvation."[1]

Therefore, if by chance you one day happen to be nailed upon a cross next to the Savior of the world, then maybe you could be excused from having to be doused with water. But then again, was the thief really excused from baptism? Was he not baptized in the least? Christ was there performing an extraordinary ritual. Yes, Christ was there, let us never forget – the One of whom it was said would baptize "with the Holy Spirit and fire." (Matt. 3:11) The sign, if there was one, would have surely faded into the darkness of the hour anyhow.

The case of the dying thief aside, in exactly what sense is forgiveness dependent upon baptism? In the sense that baptism is the door to Christ. Eternal life, or salvation – whatever you want to call it – is not merely an encounter with a person, though it certainly is that. It is an encounter with a person and his world. "Today you will be with me in paradise." (Luke 23:43) That is what is meant by a new creation. In Christ's world we find forgiveness. When we enter into the life that is in Christ, we are entering into just that – a brand new life, a brand new world. Baptism is the door to that world. That is why the Creed reads "One baptism for the remission of sins." The emphasis is on the "One", not on the "remission of sins". The remission of sins is taken for granted. It is assumed. On the contrary, it is the fact that there is only *one* baptism which works forgiveness that is revolutionary.

12
ASSURANCE

Assurance of salvation is like a treacherous mountain. Just as you make it to the summit, if you are not careful, you could slide right down the other side. Climbing it is daunting. Conquering it may seem insurmountable. In many cases, we may not even remain at the top long enough to enjoy the view. It is a long, difficult road getting there, marred by pitfalls and dangers. Sometimes the easiest way to climb is to forget you are even climbing. But it is too easy to get lost, and if we lose our bearings, we may end up back down the mountain without realizing it. When we finally do make it to the top and take in the view, provided we are able to balance upon the narrow precipice, everything we had accomplished vanishes in the revelation that the only genuine assurance of salvation comes by realizing that our salvation is thus far quite unsure.

The Christian life – the life of following Jesus – is plagued by doubts. This is quite natural, by the way. It is nothing to be afraid of. If there was nothing to doubt, then there would be no need for faith, for faith is the process of overcoming doubt with belief. If we had absolute certainty that our perception of God was grounded in reality then we would have no need for faith. We would simply know, and we would be quite sure that we knew. We would know in the same way that we know our own child's name. It would be plain to us.

But the Christian life is not like that. It is not so plain. It requires diligence. It requires experience. It requires a long, tiresome journey to reach the pinnacle and realize that it was the faith which we carried with us all along that gives us the assurance. It is not something that can be understood by reaching a state of nirvana. It is understood by reaching a state of humility. It is humility that teaches us patience. It is humility that teaches us that we are weak. It is this state of complete dependence upon God that teaches us that doubt, although a bitter enemy, must first become a friend.

Did Noah not have reason to doubt? How did he know that he was not wasting his time waiting all those of years for rain to fall? Yet he built an ark. Did Abraham not have reason to doubt? How did he know that the voice of God was not the voice of the devil? Yet he went. Did Moses's mother not have reason to doubt? After all, what are the odds of a baby surviving amongst the reeds of the Nile River? Yet she set her baby there and he delivered a nation. Faith is having reason to doubt, yet not doubting. Faith is believing despite not fully understanding. As the Word of God attests, "Faith is the substance of things hoped for, the evidence of things not seen." (Heb. 11:1) It is not as though faith is without evidence. Faith *is* the evidence when all other evidence is lacking. It is not as though faith is without substance. Faith *is* the substance when everything else is grasping at the wind. Faith is, as one translation puts it, assurance. (NASB)

God is interesting this way. He gives us all these impossible things to believe, all these unthinkable things to do. Left to ourselves, it would be enough to drive even the sagest of sages to the brink of insanity. Anyone who considers the life of God is considering a life of lunacy, a weight under which no man can bear up. But it is the only life nonetheless, and that is what makes it sane in the end. It is the only life with any lasting reward. And God is fully aware of this. He is not indifferent to our frailty. For this reason, he gives us a means of obtaining assurance. He provides a way for us to know – yes, to *know* – that the life which he requires will by no means return to us void. That is the purpose of faith. Faith is a supernatural gift. But faith will not last forever. It is given to us for a time – a time when it is crucial for us to carry it – a time when it is impossible for us to persevere under the weight of God without it, and it bears three marks of assurance in this life.

The first mark of assurance is completely inward. It is called hope. Remember, faith is the substance, or assurance, of things hoped for. Therefore, there are particular things for which we hope. Things which lay ahead. Rewards, gifts, desirable things. Things in our future, but things which we have not yet fully grasped. They are far enough away from us to remain a mystery, yet close enough that we might take a little whiff, a little taste. They are things of which we are certain, not because they make perfect sense or because they are reasonable in themselves, but because they are understood supernaturally. They are understood by faith. They are things that are promised. Things that are experienced in part, but not yet in full. They are things hoped for. Faith is the assurance of these things. Faith is being certain that the uncertain things are real.

But what about the assurance of faith? Does faith not require its own assurance? For how can we be certain that faith is genuine or that faith has the power to grasp what it is supposed to grasp? How do we know that we really have it? Faith and hope work together, for although faith is the assurance of things hoped for, hope is the assurance of faith. Hope is a quality which, though born of faith, strengthens faith. When we believe in the certain promises to be fulfilled, it is the hope of those fulfillments that gives credibility to the belief. It is the expectation, the product of faith, which gives us the assurance that faith is not in vain. That is a purely inward experience. That is God telling you that you are his. If you hope for the things promised, you can be sure that you have faith. It is for you only. Nobody else can see the hope that is within you. Sure, you can talk about it, but only you know if you possess it.

The second mark of assurance, contrary to the first, is completely outward. It is called fruit. Fruit is what faith looks like when it grows. Just as an orange tree bears oranges, a Christ tree bears Christians. If the health of an orange tree comes into question, we can learn much from examining the oranges. Healthy oranges mean a healthy tree. Unhealthy oranges mean there is a problem in the tree. Bad fruit means bad branches. In the same way, if Christian fruit is bad, it means a bad Christian.

Fruit is never examined by the thing bearing it. An apricot branch is not going to discern the apricot. It requires someone to harvest the apricot, someone to look at it, someone to taste it in order to determine whether it is useful or rotten. Fruit is always judged by those on the outside. That is why a Christian can deduce very little from examining his own fruit. "I have produced good fruit, therefore I can be sure that I am right with God." That reasoning only produces pride. Then, in order to combat pride, the Christian, if he is honest with himself, will decide, "The fruit I have produced is not the best, in fact, it is often rotten, therefore I cannot be sure that I am right with God." Is this reasoning any better? The optimistic self-examination returns prideful. The honest self-examination returns despondent. No, examination of the fruit must never be done by the one being examined as a means of gaining assurance.

But please do not misunderstand. I do not mean to assert that self-examination is never beneficial in any way. Certainly, in some ways it can be. Certainly we must test ourselves to determine whether we are living the way we ought to be living. Certainly we should search inside of ourselves and take inventory of our spiritual condition. But self-examination is not for the purpose of gaining assurance. Our fruit is for others to judge. Such is evident when Jesus said, "By this all will know that you are My disciples, if you have love for one another."(John 13.35) Notice that he did not say that we will know *ourselves* by our love, but that others will know us. Instead, we judge ourselves according to the hope which lies within us. Questioning our hope is also part of the self-examination process, but trying to discern our own fruit is like an artist judging his own art, or a pitcher judging his own fastball. He is likely to either think it is the greatest thing on the face of the earth or that it is a disaster. No, we cannot gain assurance from examining our own fruit. Good fruit is required by God, but it is not given to us as a checklist in order to determine our good standing with him. Examining our own fruit as a means of assurance, if we are honest, will only drive us to despair, or at the very least, frustration. The dire reality is that bad fruit can certainly give us reason to doubt our right standing with God, but good fruit will never justify self confidence in the same. At no time can you look at your productivity and say, "I know that God must be pleased." We are damned if we don't, and quite possibly damned if we do. But others may judge us. The church may judge us. Even the world may judge us. Yet self-examination is useful in that if it causes you to doubt your good standing with the Savior, if you are mindful of the sinfulness of your sin and have trouble believing that God's grace has found you, then do not be afraid to draw upon the judgments of others.

The third mark of assurance bears directly upon our topic at hand. It differs from the first two in that it is applicable to each of us personally as well as to those who observe us. It is both an inward as well as an outward means of assurance. It is called baptism. Baptism, being that it testifies to what God has done for us, has the power to assure us that his grace is really ours; that first of all, salvation is real, and secondly, that we really do partake in the salvation. In other words, baptism teaches us that God saves us.

We have already dealt in part with this phenomenal aspect of baptism in earlier sections, but we have not necessarily dealt with *how* something so objective, how a short ceremonial washing can become to us the grace of knowing that God is at work in our lives to save us from an eternity of damnation. What is it about baptism that communicates this amazing assurance of salvation?

To be clear, assurance does not come from the baptism itself but from what it represents – no, more than represents – from what it does. Baptism communicates, or carries, like a pigeon carries a message, a declaration by God that we have been forgiven. It is not the baptism that forgives us. It merely works the forgiveness. The forgiveness comes from divine promise. Baptism acts as a carrier of those promises. It links us to God in a visible, tangible way so that we might believe – so that we might know! – that God is gracious to save us. Remember, baptism is a sign – but not only a sign – it is a seal of the covenant of grace that God made with Abraham, purchased and secured through Jesus Christ on our behalf for our eternal life. Therefore, baptism is a reliable messenger of the promise of salvation. The promises of God are attached to the baptism because baptism is a sacrament, just as the Westminster Confession of Faith notes, "There is, in every sacrament, a spiritual relation, or a sacramental union, between the sign and the thing signified."[1] Furthermore, Luther's catechism states that "A sacrament is a sacred act instituted by God in which God himself has joined His Word of promise to a visible element…"[2] Though faith and repentance are essential to any person's salvation, baptism is a work of God which unites us to the prior work that Christ has already done on our behalf in making atonement for us. In this sense, baptism, as a sacrament, sparks, feeds, and nurtures faith. Baptism is a breeding ground for a lifetime of faith. Though it is not sufficient to bring salvation to completion, it is sufficient to assure us that God loves us and made a sacrifice of atonement for our sins. Is that not a wonderful grace to fall back upon?

Now some will say wait a minute. One objector will complain that such a high view of baptism will certainly lead many to rely upon the water instead of upon God, resulting in a false assurance. Another objector will complain that in such a high view of baptism faith is not given its proper place. These are really not two objections, but one. The complaint originates from a misunderstanding regarding the relationship between baptism and faith, or baptism and discipleship. Someone who is baptized in ignorance must be taught to believe. Faith is something that is learned, is it not? But some will say no, faith is a supernatural act of God. It is a gift. This is true, but so is baptism. Baptism is no less a supernatural act of God than is faith. In fact, just as baptisms may be misused or contrived, so might faith. There is no difference. Faith is a supernatural act of God born out of the promises in his Word. Baptism, as a carrier of those promises, acts in the same manner as his Word does – it nurtures faith. So the person who is baptized, if he is taught to use the sacrament correctly, will look upon his baptism as he will look upon the Word of God, as a declaration of the gospel. When he does this, is that not faith? If a person looks to his baptism for assurance of salvation, why are we so quick to rebuke him as a legalist when the very baptism he looks to is communicating the very promises of assurance found in God's Word?

This is the same principle that is found in children. Children may learn to pray the Lord's Prayer, but they may not always know the significance of the words. Children may learn a hymn, but not necessarily know its meaning. This does not negate the fact that they are praying and singing. They are merely children. They grow up. They learn. But the larger amount of knowledge that they will obtain later on does not negate the small amount of knowledge which they possess in the beginning. It is still faith, but faith which requires improving. Adult converts are the same way. When a man is born of God and baptized, his faith requires improving. The process of doing this is called discipleship. Baptism should never take place apart from discipleship. It is true that if baptism is left by itself as grounds for the hope of one's salvation, the salvation rests upon very shaky ground indeed. But when baptism is used rightly, it becomes a beautiful picture of what God has done in Christ through the Holy Spirit, and it becomes a means of assurance that we belong to Christ and that we are perfectly secure in his loving, faithful salvation.

Therefore, baptism is a sign for us personally as well as for others. When we struggle with sin or doubt or forget that God's grace is for us, we remember our baptism and trust that God has washed all the filth away, making us clean. When we begin to stray or disobey or worry that Christ's way is too difficult, we remember our baptism and know that we must repent because we no longer belong to ourselves, but to God. Baptism is a sign for others because they are reminded that we are all one in Christ. When I become bothersome or burdensome, they will remember my baptism and receive me into the fellowship. They will help bear my burdens. They will overlook my bothers. They will help save me from my sins. They cannot turn away, because I, like them, have received the grace of God in baptism.

With all that being said, you might still ask, "What are these divine promises that baptism carries? For if there are no promises, then all this talk is really in vain." Well, there are many, but this one is sufficient. Mark 16:16 promises that "He who believes and is baptized will be saved, but he who does not believe will be condemned." This is why Luther, in his catechism, says of baptism that "It works the forgiveness of sins, rescues from death and the devil, and gives eternal salvation to all who believe this, as the words and promises of God declare."(3)

If baptism is used apart from faith, then it is used incorrectly and no true assurance can be derived from it. This is not to say, however, that faith must precede baptism – on the contrary. Baptism is God planting faith. Baptism is God strengthening faith. When baptism is used correctly, it assumes faith, for only the eyes of faith will look upon baptism and see something besides water. They will see the grace of God.

13
WASHING OF REGENERATION

"But when the kindness and the love of God our Savior toward man appeared, not by works of righteousness which we have done, but according to His mercy He saved us, through the washing of regeneration and renewing of the Holy Spirit, whom he poured out on us abundantly through Jesus Christ our Savior, that having been justified by His grace we should become heirs according to the hope of eternal life." (Titus 3:4-7)

In our modern theological discourses, mentioning baptism in the same breath as regeneration is like walking through a landmine. You never know when you are going to get blown to pieces. It is the taboo of all taboos. It is the king of taboos. If you mention baptismal regeneration as a serious possibility (meaning in any other manner besides a joke or with a scowl across your brow) you will most likely have to duck for cover or find a hole to crawl into. At worst, you will be tried for heresy. At best, you will be called a Lutheran.

Regeneration, however, according to the Apostle, is a washing. Granted, there is no mention of water in this particular text, but do not let that omission trick you into forgetting that, according to the Apostle, regeneration is a washing. The implication of this exhortation in Paul's epistle to Titus is to draw a connection between regeneration and baptism, or more directly between baptism and the life giving work of the Holy Spirit. Look closely at the text.

First of all, regeneration is likened to a washing. This is evident from the words, "the washing of regeneration." Secondly, regeneration is shown to be a work which is performed by the Holy Spirit. This is evident by the fact that this concept of the Holy Spirit being the one who regenerates is held universally among Christians. It is denied essentially nowhere. But if that is not enough, the words "renewing of the Holy Spirit" being given in connection with "the washing of regeneration" should be sufficient proof. Therefore, if we can safely agree that regeneration is a washing and that regeneration is performed by the Holy Spirit, we can conclude that the washing in view here is a work performed by the Holy Spirit. But is it baptism? Does Paul have baptism in mind when he mentions "the washing of regeneration and renewing of the Holy Spirit?" Or does he have another kind of washing in mind? Something that does not involve water, or ritual, or cleansing?

One possibility is that Paul is simply using the concept of washing as a metaphor for the regenerating work of the Holy Spirit. The emphasis is on the Holy Spirit, you might say. Therefore, he is primarily referring to a spiritual phenomenon, or what you might call being born again. This regeneration, or new birth, is being done directly, straight from God without the use of any physical means, and the concept of washing is only used to describe the results of this inward work of the Holy Spirit rather than the means in which this work of the Holy Spirit takes place. Could this not be what the Apostle is really trying to communicate?

I think the answer is really even simpler than that. Why must we be so quick to drive a wedge between the spiritual work of God and the physical means that God uses to bring about his spiritual work? Yes, Paul is certainly using the concept of washing as a metaphor for the regenerating work of the Holy Spirit, but, remember, sacraments are metaphors. Sacraments are physical elements which communicate spiritual phenomenon. They are elements around which heaven and earth collide. Why would Paul use the metaphor of washing to describe regeneration? What logical connection exists between washing and being born anew? When someone considers the renewing work of the Holy Spirit, the giving of new life where there was previously death, does the concept of washing come to mind? Will cleaning a corpse bring it back to life again? If Paul uses the concept of washing merely as a metaphor for regeneration apart from any physical means, then Paul could have chosen a much better one – one that at least makes sense.

Let's consider Paul's words to Titus in light of God's words to a wayward Israel through the prophet Ezekiel:

"For I will take you from among the nations, gather you out of all countries, and bring you into your own land. Then I will sprinkle clean water on you, and you shall be clean; I will cleanse you from all your filthiness and from all your idols. I will give you a new heart and put a new spirit within you; I will take the heart of stone out of your flesh and give you a heart of flesh. I will put my Spirit within you and cause you to walk in My statutes, and you will keep My judgments and do them. Then you shall dwell in the land that I gave to your fathers; you shall be My people, and I will be your God. I will deliver you from all your uncleanness." (Ez. 36:24-29)

The language used by Ezekiel is similar to the language used by Jeremiah when Jeremiah describes the new covenant that God will make with the house of Israel. We will examine that text in later chapters, but notice first the similarities between this portion of Scripture and that in the letter to Titus. Notice how both refer to the cleansing that is the work of the Holy Spirit. The difference is that Ezekiel makes clear that this cleansing, this renewal, accompanies a washing with water. God reiterates his covenant to his people, and he does it through a cleansing ritual in which he gives his Spirit to his wayward children so that they will turn from their idolatry and follow the statues of the Lord. This is not insignificant. What God is revealing through Ezekiel in alluding to a new covenant which is to come, Paul is echoing to Titus by reminding him that God has definitely accomplished this salvation through the work of Jesus Christ and applied it to his people through the washing of regeneration and renewing of the Holy Spirit. Is this not why Nicodemus was rebuked by Christ? For not understanding this connection?

It was nightfall, and Nicodemus, a teacher of the law, came sneaking up to Jesus. He was curious. He wanted to confront Jesus in the darkness. Was his curiosity sincere? When he acknowledged that Jesus was from God, did he really believe it or was it mere flattery? I do not know, but Jesus apparently knew more about his motives than that which comes across in the text. Jesus immediately throws a mental roadblock before Nicodemus. He tells Nicodemus that he must be re-born if he is to have any hope in seeing the kingdom of God. Nicodemus was thrown for a loop. Surely he expected some discussion on the matters of the law or maybe in the restoration of the theocracy, but Jesus stops him abruptly before he even has a chance to spin the conversation out of control. Nicodemus appears flabbergasted, almost at a loss for thought, and can only ask "How?" Maybe he thought he was being smart when he questioned Jesus about entering a second time into his mother's womb, or maybe he was sincerely wondering, but regardless, he was met once again by the striking words of Christ: "Most assuredly, I say to you, unless one is born of water and the Spirit, he cannot enter the Kingdom of God." When Nicodemus again answered, "How can these things be?" Jesus rebuked him by saying, "Are you the teacher of Israel, and do not know these things?" As a student of the prophets, Nicodemus should have known. He should have understood how God works through water. He should have known about the Holy Spirit. Though baptism had not yet been instituted as a sacrament of the church, it was still part of the ritual, and Nicodemus should have discerned this. (John 3:1-18)

"Unless one is born of water and the Spirit, he cannot enter the kingdom of God." Jesus is saying nothing less than what was prophesied by Ezekiel. Jesus was saying nothing less than what was later indicated by Paul. The door to the kingdom which is established in Christ's blood is the cleansing work of the Holy Spirit. The cleansing work of the Holy Spirit is wrought through the waters of baptism. Again, there is no power in the water. The water is a physical means by which the Holy Spirit distributes the blessings, or the promises, of God's Word. Jesus was telling Nicodemus that he must become a new creation if he is to see God's kingdom.

Where did this subjective notion of regeneration that we have become so acquainted with first arise? Why, when we think of being born again, do we assume it means in the depths of our being? Christ came to establish a kingdom. The kingdom he came to establish is visible. It has real properties and elements and can be seen moving, advancing, developing in the world. The kingdom of God has a physical presence upon earth. It is not far removed from our senses. Nicodemus understood at least this much. In fact, it seems he may have understood more than our modern churches do. He, like every other Israelite, expected a physical kingdom with a flesh and blood king living and moving upon the earth and going to battle and throwing off the yoke of slavery for all the people. Nicodemus at least expected that much. The problem was that Jesus' proposal was too spiritual for him. So why, then, has it become too physical for us?

Jesus was telling Nicodemus that the world was about to change. There was a cataclysmic event that was taking place in which Heaven was colliding with earth in the person of Christ. The words "you must be born again" were not so much in reference to an inner change that must first take place in Nicodemus, but rather, an eschatological change which was about to take place in the world. Regeneration is new life in the person of Jesus Christ, not in the person of Nicodemus. But the person of Nicodemus must enter that life if he is to have any hope of living. Nicodemus was far too outwardly focused to see that kingdom. The modern church appears too inwardly focused to tell the difference. "You must be born of water and the Spirit." In other words, you must enter the kingdom through the washing of the Holy Spirit.

When Paul writes to Titus, "He saved us, through the washing of regeneration and renewing of the Holy Spirit…" he is referring to a comprehensive view of salvation. So often we think of salvation as if we are making a bank withdrawal. We go to the bank, we make the transaction – and BOOM – we get everything we need all at once. On the contrary, Paul, throughout his epistles, articulates a much more elastic understanding of salvation, not so much as a process, nor as a progression, but more of a prolonged experience, a comprehensive drama of which baptism is an essential ingredient. He presents ideas like "Having believed, you were sealed with the Holy Spirit of promise, who is the guarantee of our inheritance until the redemption of the purchased possession," (Eph. 1.13-14) or "Now He who establishes us with you in Christ and has anointed us is God, who also has sealed us and given us the Spirit in our hearts as a guarantee." (2 Cor. 1.21-23)

There is that word again, *seal.* Remember that concept? These ideas imply something further. Something which is waiting. Waiting to be taken hold of at the right time. The giving of the Spirit in regeneration is a seal; it is not the end-all in regards to our salvation. It is a seal in a similar way that circumcision was a seal for Abraham, a seal of the righteousness of God. There are more pieces to the puzzle. There is room for doubt and hope. There is room for growth and frustration. There is room for things much greater than we have ever experienced before, and these things are being held for us until the time is proper for them to be revealed, and it is the Holy Spirit, through the washing of regeneration, which guarantees those things for us.

Is baptism not in play here? Does Paul not have baptism in mind when he writes about washing and seals and guarantees and new life? Does it not make sense to have baptism in view when Paul asks the Galatians, "Are you so foolish? Having begun in the Spirit, are you now being made perfect by the flesh?" (Gal. 3,3) Was he not chastising them for reverting to the laws of circumcision rather than the gospel of the Spirit that was begun in baptism as a testimony to the faith of Jesus Christ? Remember, circumcision is still required, but it is a circumcision of the heart which counts, that covenant being applied to us in water baptism.

If we mean by regeneration a light switching on inside of us which kills the old man and creates a new one, like being hit by a lightning bolt, then baptism does not accomplish that ipso facto. But if we mean by regeneration emerging from out of the darkness into the light of a brand new kingdom where promises of inheritance are held out for us if we only persevere in the faith, like opening the door of a dark room and stepping out of it into a world of sunshine, then yes, baptism accomplishes this. This is what is meant, I think, by the "washing of regeneration and renewing of the Holy Spirit." This is what is meant, I think, by Jesus's words to Nicodemus. We should not be ashamed to speak in this way, for after all, it is the figure of speech used in the Scriptures as well as the confessions.

For instance, The Book of Common Prayer insists that baptism is union with Christ in his resurrection, "birth" into the church, and "new life in the Holy Spirit," as well as stating that baptism is a "sign of regeneration or new-birth, whereby, as by an instrument, they that receive baptism are rightly grafted into the church."[1] Similarly, the Westminsters confess that baptism is to be a sign and seal of our regeneration and ingrafting into Christ, [2] or in another place calling it a sign and seal of "regeneration by His Spirit, adoption, and resurrection unto everlasting life."[3]

Furthermore, in Luther's catechism, when he asks, "Why do the Scriptures call baptism the washing of rebirth and renewal of the Holy Spirit?" he answers, "In Baptism, the Holy Spirit works faith and so creates in us new spiritual life with the power to overcome sin."(4)

Whatever it is about the words 'baptism' and 'regeneration' going together that makes us uncomfortable, whatever it is about it that gives us hives and makes us sweat, whatever it is about it that bullies our perfectly worked-out theology of conversion, whatever it is must be at least revisited, for the language is the language of the Scriptures, and the language is the language of the churches, and no matter how distasteful it might be upon our palates, it still does not compromise our precious insistence that an inward quickening must always precede justification or that faith is a gift of the Holy Spirit. Salvation is the gospel at work in the world, and it is not always so easy to articulate upon the head of a pin. Rather, it works itself out over the course of a lifetime of complexities. It is this comprehensive understanding of salvation, this drama that should drive us more readily to our knees in fear and thankfulness, frustration and awe, humility and utter dependence upon God.

14
BAPTISM AND THE WARDROBE

Imagine for a moment the Pevensie (1) children in that great big house, playing games, running all about looking for a place to hide from one another, and imagine Lucy, that despite her haste to rush into the wardrobe, her curiosity getting the better of her, stops to inquire instead of a dresser drawer, the dresser standing solitary in the corner of the room. Imagine that she forgets for a moment about the wardrobe. Imagine that she reaches for the top drawer and pulls it open thinking that she might find beautiful jewelry or fashionable clothing. Imagine her surprise when she instead pulls out a well preserved book, no doubt ancient, and her young mind immediately forgets all about hide-and-go-seek and the wardrobe, being drawn into the curious world of Narnia by another means altogether, by the words of a book.

Imagine that she held in her hands an ancient account of Narnia, a testimony written by the creatures of Narnia, the very testimony of Aslan himself. It would tell of the creation of Narnia, all the battles, the victories and the defeats. It would lay claim to the history of the animals, to the rise and fall of the kings and princes, of deliverance and betrayal. It would tell how Aslan sacrifices himself upon the great stone table as a ransom for a troublesome little boy – yes, even for a Pevensie– and how a witch would henceforth be destroyed. It would tell of a world of peace, a world worth fighting for, a hope for the future, a judgment day, and an eternal kingdom. Imagine that Lucy took hold of this book and read it. Imagine that she believed it, not as some mythical allegory, but as mythical truth and history, as a real testimony of another world. Imagine that she took this book and showed it to the other children. Suppose they believed it too? Then what?

I suppose that it would be of great benefit to them. I suppose that they would come to know Aslan, that mighty lion and creator of the world. I suppose they would find great comfort in knowing that Narnia was their world too, that they are a part of it, even to the point of becoming kings and queens. They would have a relationship with Aslan, no doubt, for he would speak to them in this testimony, and they would hear his words by faith. They would be a part of Narnia, and Narnia would be a part of them. They would gain great affection for the other world – thinking about it, dreaming about it, playing about it, and yes, longing for it, for it would only exist in a book – a real book to be sure, but a book nonetheless, and although it would be of great benefit to them to learn and understand their true place in Narnia and their true relationship with Aslan, it could never take them there, not until – yes, not until they did that one thing, that one thing about from which Lucy had been distracted – they must enter the wardrobe.

Of course! It is only by entering the wardrobe that they can exit through the other side. It is only by entering the wardrobe that they enter into Narnia. It is only by entering the wardrobe that they can experience the new world for themselves. Apart from the wardrobe, they are believers in a distant country, but through the wardrobe they become citizens, not only by believing the testimony, but physically, by really living there in the kingdom of Aslan. And not only so, but they will meet him face to face, and the world of which they had only read about in the book becomes not only a comfort to them but an experience as well, for they can see the snow fall, they can taste the food, they can watch the flowers bloom and hear animals talking. It is in Narnia where the adventures begin. It is the wardrobe by which they gain access. It is the wardrobe where two worlds, two realities, collide.

15
THE SAVING POWER OF BAPTISM

Let's revisit for a moment Paul's words to Titus. Regarding this Scripture, it is no little thing to note that Paul is writing concerning matters of salvation. He tells Titus that "according to His great mercy He saved us, through the washing of regeneration…" (Titus 3:4-7) This washing, Paul reasons, actually saved them.

It is one thing to say that baptism makes Christians by bringing converts into the body of Christ. It is one thing to say that in baptism, the promise of forgiveness is offered and even sealed for the recipient. It is one thing to say that baptism is real union with Christ. It is one thing to say that baptism provides assurance of salvation. It is even one thing to say that baptism is a sign of regeneration for the recipient. Yes, it is one thing to say that baptism is gospel and that it communicates many great benefits of faith. But salvation itself? Yes, it is one thing to affirm that baptism does all these things, but it is quite another to affirm that baptism saves us. Is it not?

Paul says we are saved by the washing of regeneration. Christ says that if you believe and are baptized then you will be saved. And Peter says to repent and be baptized for the forgiveness of our sins. But Peter says something else as well. He says something else under the inspiration of the Holy Spirit. He says that baptism saves us. He says, "There is also an antitype which now saves us – baptism (not the removal of the filth of the flesh, but the answer of a good conscience toward God), through the resurrection of Jesus Christ." (1 Pet. 3:20-22)

This baptism of which he refers is water baptism – real, visible, water baptism. This is not an invisible baptism. This is not the work of the Holy Spirit apart from water. This is something verifiable. It can be seen with the eyes and felt on the body. We know this because it is being compared to the real water by which Noah was saved. Baptism is called an antitype. An antitype is the fulfillment of the shadow. It is the real thing. It is the fullness of what was prefigured in the past. In this case, Noah's flood prefigured the baptism which now saves us, the flood being a type or shadow; water baptism being the antitype. The flood was the blueprint; baptism is the house.

Noah was saved through real, verifiable water. He watched it come down from the heavens. He watched it rise up from the depths. Peter tells us that this flood saved Noah – No, not only Noah – this flood saved eight souls in all. They were saved *through* the water, that pounding, pouring, rising, dangerous water, water which killed an entire world except for eight souls, a deluge of death and destruction. This flood immersed the entire world, but God saved Noah because he escaped by way of an ark; he and his wife, and his sons and their wives. They entered in and God shut them up inside. And the ark was rocked and tossed and carried about by the wrestling waves, but eight souls were safe inside with God. (Gen. Ch. 6-7) That is the shadow. That is what Peter wants us to understand as the figure pointing to a future fulfillment. The flood waters brought destruction for some and salvation to others, blessed salvation for those who were safe inside the ark. Peter tells us that this is what baptism is like. It is the passing through the waters of God's judgment and being kept safe with him in the ark. In this way, baptism saves us.

Peter makes an interesting distinction, however. He is careful to note that it is not in washing the filth from the flesh that baptism saves us, but rather, it is the pledge of a good conscience toward God. This is further evidence that water baptism is in view.

It is not the cleansing of the skin through the washing of water that has power, but rather, it is the pledge, or the testimony, which confirms the salvation. As it is written in the confessions, "Sacraments ordained of Christ be not only badges or tokens of Christian men's profession, but rather they be certain sure witnesses, and effectual signs of grace…"(1) This emphasis on the pledge of a good conscience toward God is no proof that the salvation in view comes apart from water baptism, but on the contrary. Peter is making this distinction in order to show what baptism actually does. It saves us, not simply by virtue of water running down the skin, but by virtue of the testimony which it represents. Baptism is a covenant ritual. It is a cleansing ritual. It is the work of God the Holy Spirit. It is God's testimony, not man's. It is God's pledge, not mine. It is God's flood, not Noah's. This is how it can be said that baptism now saves us. It saves exactly the same way that I have been harping upon all along – that in baptism, all the promises and hopes of God for salvation are bound up and carried by the Holy Spirit, confirmed, and distributed. In baptism, God says "You are mine! Repent and believe!"

Though it sounds contrary to so much of the teaching we presently encounter, particularly salvation by grace alone, it should not surprise us when the Augsburg Confession mentions that baptism is necessary for salvation, for certainly this is really no different than what the Westminster Confession mentions when it states that the church is "…the house and family of God, *out of which there is no ordinary possibility of salvation.*"(2) To say that baptism is necessary for salvation and that there is no assurance of salvation outside the church is really to say the same thing. Again, if we take these words to mean that all one has to do to secure eternal life is go to the pastor and get dunked or have water poured over our heads or our children's heads, then we have not even come close to understanding the significance of baptism. At the same time, if we are unable to see the connection between water baptism and all these glorious benefits of salvation which are so wonderfully articulated for us in the Scriptures and in the confessions, then in this we have also failed to understand the significance of baptism. Baptism, as a means of grace, delivers grace. Grace comes by way of the Holy Spirit. Baptism is not works righteousness. It testifies to God's righteousness. Baptism is not man centered. It is Christ centered. Baptism is not man's work. It is God's work. If we understand baptism in any other way than it being God's testimony rather than man's, then we will fail immediately in our application of it. That is why we can honestly say like Peter, and like Paul, and like Jesus that baptism saves, because we can honestly say that God saves.

PART THREE

CHILDREN IN THE CHURCH

16
A HOUSE FOR MY NAME

I have thus far attempted to answer two questions; the first being 'What is baptism?' and the second being 'What does baptism do?' The answer to the first is that baptism is a sacrament of the church, a cleansing ritual of gospel inclusion. The answer to the second is that baptism is used by the Holy Spirit to communicate and distribute various graces of the gospel call. The occasion has arrived in which to move forward. With the nature and function of baptism now in our back pocket, it is time to address weightier matters, matters of practice. It is time to wade into the murky waters of unity and attempt to clean it up a bit, for that is the purpose of this book after all, no matter how presumptuous or impossible it might seem. It is time to address the question 'For whom is baptism intended?' or to put it another way, 'Should infants and children be baptized?' No, that does not suffice, for being that baptism is initiation into the church, the doorway through which one is to enter the kingdom of Heaven, the question must be put even more directly than that – 'Are infants and children members of the body of Christ?' Yes, that is the question. That is the question upon which the practice of baptizing children hinges. Let us attempt to answer that question as we consider the proper use of baptism and the problem of disunity in the church.

There is a reason that King David is called a man after God's own heart. It is not because he was brave in battle. It is not because he was morally pure or, on the contrary, sensitive of his own sinfulness. It was not because of his obedience. David is considered a man after God's own heart because he *got* it. David's vision for life was so fused with God's will that he was accurately called a man after God's own heart. When God spoke, David listened – and he not only listened – he *got* it. He understood. And once he understood, there was no stopping him. He was God's hand upon this earth. He was God's heart beating amidst his people.

Such is the case one day when David was in his palace. Maybe he was sitting, maybe reclining, no doubt admiring the handiwork of the architecture, no doubt thinking about God. He was probably thankful. He was probably in awe. He was probably considering why the Almighty would choose him of all people, a mere shepherd boy, to become the ruler of his nation, to become the object of his affection, the recipient of unimaginable wealth and prosperity. He was probably enjoying some peace and quiet when he thought, 'Why? Why am I allowed to enjoy this beautiful house when it is the Lord alone who is worthy of such honor?' So he did what any well intentioned man would do. He told his prophet that he wanted to build a house for God. His prophet told him, "Do all that is in your heart, for the Lord is with you." Then God stepped in. God said not so fast. God said no you won't. (2 Sam. Ch. 7)

Is this not just like us? When we contemplate all that God has done, are we not then tempted to do something for God in return? After all, we love him, right? We appreciate the blessings from his hand, and we want to reciprocate. We are tempted to become restless despite the rest that he gives us. Sometimes it is not that simple, however. Sometimes we consider all that God has done for us and we feel guilty because we know that we have not done enough for him, as if we could outdo God. But that is our inclination. We think that maybe by doing this one thing we could justify all that we have already been so graciously given. We feel that God's grace isn't good enough, or maybe more accurately that we are not good enough for his grace, so we try to compensate. We forget what grace is. We forget that everything is God's to begin with. I am not sure as to David's motivation, but one thing is clear.

David was enjoying God's blessings and felt that God was in some manner deprived. He felt that God needed at least a house as nice as his own.

But God said something remarkable, something that sent David to his knees, something that would change the way David would think about the future. God spoke, and David *got* it. God said essentially two things. First, he said, 'No, David. You will not build me a house, but I will build *you* one.' (2 Sam. 7.11) God was reminding David that *he* alone is the benefactor, that you cannot out-give God. God was reminding David that God alone is in possession of all blessings, that "The earth is the Lord's and all its fullness." (Ps. 24.1) It is not for us to judge the needs of God, for God does as he pleases. God does not need man to increase his status, for his glory is already established upon the earth. God was teaching David this certainly, but God was teaching David something else as well, something deeper, something more mysterious.

God was establishing David's seed, his offspring, one who was to come from his own body, to rule over the kingdom forever. God was telling David that although he had already given him a kingdom in which to rule and a palace in which to live, and although it was David's desire to give back to God by building him something great, that David had not even begun to imagine the blessings that were still in store, that God was not finished yet. In fact, God was not only about to establish the rule of David while he was alive, but he was promising to establish that rule of David long after he would be dead. God was telling him that "When your days are fulfilled and you rest with your fathers, I will set up your seed after you, who will come from your body, and I will establish his kingdom. He shall build a house for My name, and I will establish the throne of his kingdom forever." (2 Sam. 7.12-13)

So here is David who wanted to build something great for his Lord, being told by God that God was going to build something even greater for him. Here is God blessing David even further than he already had while at the same time establishing for himself greater glory than David could have ever possibly returned to him.

This promise of God to David has come to be called the Davidic covenant. It is the promise that God will make David's name great, that God will build for him a house and will establish through him a kingdom everlasting. How was David to understand this? I think he understood this in the plainest sense possible. He did not try to rationalize it or mythologize or allegorize it. He heard it and believed it. He understood that God would never wipe his name from the face of the earth. He understood that God would not abandon him to the grave. He understood that long after he was gone, he would continue to live. That is what he understood. That is how he *got* it. That was why he was called a man after God's own heart.

But there was something else that God was saying as well. By indicating that God would build *David* a house instead of the other way around, God was not implying that a house for himself would not be built. On the contrary, God acknowledged that he wanted his own house built but that it would not be David who would build it. It would be his seed, one from his own body who would do this. "He shall build a house for My name, and I will establish the throne of his kingdom forever." Not only was God telling David not to get ahead of himself, not only was he telling David that he would establish David's house forever, but he was telling him that a house would be built for God, but that David would not be the one to do it; rather, it would be built by one "who will come from your body."

We know in the most obvious sense whom God was referring to, for David had a son named Solomon and the day came, after "David rested with his fathers and was buried in the city of David," that "Solomon sat on the throne of his father David; and his kingdom was firmly established." (1 Kin. 2.10-12) We know that it was Solomon who built the temple of the Lord. He began building in the fourth year of his reign for he remembered what God had spoken to his father, David. Therefore, God's Word was fulfilled through Solomon. This is true, but this is not all. David was not called a man after God's own heart merely because he accepted that God wanted Solomon to build the temple instead of himself. No, when David understood these words of God, he understood something even greater. He understood that although it was Solomon of whom God spoke, it was not *only* Solomon of whom God spoke. It was the fact that David himself would never cease to be. It was that his seed would endure, and that seed is the King of Israel. It is David's own offspring who would rule, and in so doing, David would rule, but not in the power of man. This was no natural kingship. It was clearly supernatural in the mind of David, for when David heard God say, "Your throne has been established forever," (2 Sam. 7.16) he understood that to mean *forever*, and it brought him to his knees. It brought him to his knees because he understood God's promise in the context of God's covenant with Abraham. It brought him to his knees because he understood it in the context of none other than the promised Christ. If God promised Abraham that through Abraham God would establish nations for himself, then God promised David that through David God would establish a "House for My name."

17
YOU AND YOUR CHILDREN

What is this house to which God refers? Is it the house that Solomon built? Is it the temple? Is that what made David so excited? Was David brought to his knees by the thought of his son building a temple? Or was it something more? Something lasting? Something otherworldly?

We return once again to that brave apostle, fisherman Peter, the man of whom Christ said he would make a fisher of men. It was the Day of Pentecost after Jesus's crucifixion. A multitude of Jews had gathered from among the nations. There, the Holy Spirit made his presence known. He came upon them in power, like the sound of a rushing wind, causing many of them to speak in a foreign tongue, a tongue which was understood in the various languages of the people. The congregation was amazed and perplexed. Just as God at one time scattered the people of the earth by the division of language (Gen. 11.7-9), he was now bringing them together by the multiplication of the same. (Acts 2.1-12) Just as God brought confusion in the days of Babel, he was bringing confusion on the Day of Pentecost, only this time the confusion brought unity rather than discord.

In the midst of the confusion and the apparent drunkenness, Peter takes the opportunity to straighten everything out. He tells the crowd that this is not an issue of drunkenness, but rather, the Holy Spirit is being poured out right before their very eyes. (Acts 2.17-20; Joel 2.28-32) Then he preaches. Powerfully, he preaches. Amazingly, of all things, he takes the opportunity to expound upon the Davidic covenant – that covenant that God made with King David as he sat in his palace devising a scheme to build a house for God. Peter is telling the congregation all about that house. But it is not a house that David built. Nor is it a house that Solomon built. It is a house that God built. It is called the house of Israel. It is a house for God's name.

In explaining this covenant, Peter appeals first to David's faith that God would fulfill this promise through him and that his throne would be established forever. This is apparent in his reference to Psalm 16. (Acts 2.25-28) Peter mentions that David fully expected that his soul would not die, that his flesh would not "see corruption." When David penned the words of Psalm 16, it was as if it was in direct response to the promise: "Your house and your kingdom shall be established forever before you." David believed he would live even though he would die. That is how he could honestly write about himself, "Nor will you allow your Holy One to see corruption," because it was not only about himself that he wrote – David understood that although he would die, there would come another from his own body who would live. David was referencing the coming of Christ. David was living vicariously through his offspring, and Peter says that David's faith was justified, and not only that, but it was being fulfilled right before their very eyes.

Jesus Christ, raised from the dead, was the hope of King David. He was the hope of David and he was the hope of the house of Israel. That house is the "House for My name" of which God spoke. (Acts 2.36) But as was evidenced by the phenomenon at Pentecost, it was not only the house of Israel, but it was what Christ himself called "My church." (Matt. 16.18) Yes, the promised house that God would build for himself, the house that he would build for David, was nothing less than the building of the church, the fulfillment of God's promise to Abraham. The church is to be established in the seed of David, by the one who would come from his own body, that David would live and reign only in the One who is to live and reign forever, the Lord Jesus Christ. This is what Peter is saying. But this is not *only* what Peter is saying. There is something else, something more. Peter is saying that the Holy Spirit is the fulfillment of the Davidic covenant. Peter is saying that what they experienced right there at Pentecost was the fulfillment of God's promise to David, the building of the church, and that it was in the outpouring of the Holy Spirit that the promise to David was coming to pass. (Acts 2:33)

Let's slow down a minute. I don't want to out-jump my ability to recover. After all, we are supposed to be discussing baptism, not David. So let's not get too far ahead of ourselves and take a moment to consider the results of Peter's sermon. To put it succinctly, Peter tells the house of Israel that "God has made this Jesus, whom you crucified, both Lord and Christ." This message cut the congregation to the heart, convicting them deeply, and when they cried out for answers, Peter told them, "Repent and let every one of you be baptized in the name of Jesus Christ for the remission of sins; and you shall receive the gift of the Holy Spirit. For the promise is to you and your children, and to all who are afar off, as many as the Lord our God will call." (Acts 2:36-39)

We learn a couple of things from these words of Peter. First, we learn that we are annexed to our offspring so that their reputation in some measure becomes ours. This is partly what is intrinsic in the vicarious nature of faith as evidenced in David taking comfort that his reign would be established in the reign of future generations. There is a sense in which those who come after us are known and called by the names and reputations of those who went before us. This is the outworking of a covenantal mentality, an assumption of union between one and another. It is assumed that there is a link between father and child, between mother and child, first in the roles of stewardship that have been entrusted to those positions, but also in matters of nature and procreation. A son is in some ways like his father both because he is raised and taught by his father as well as being of his father's substance. The same is true about mothers. Those who are generated from another, though not inseparably linked, are linked nonetheless to the person from whom they have come. Therefore, in this sense, David knew that his reputation, though he did much to promote it in his own life, would be established even more so by the reputation of the One who came after him. Just as a delinquent son brings reproach upon the name of his father, so an excellent son brings glory to his father's name. David took great comfort in knowing that his fortunes rested in the hands of One who would come after him, One from his own body, and delighted in the thought of living vicariously in that One.

But there is another application that comes by way of vicarious faith. It is in the hope that God will reward one on account of his regard for another. This is a concept that is absolutely evident in the pages of Scripture. God spared Lot out of his regard for Abraham. (Gen. 19.29) God spared Noah's sons out of his regard for Noah. (Gen. 7.1) In fact, Jesus healed a number of children out of regard for the faith of their parents.(1) This is an absolute principle found in God's Word; that God blesses some people on account of others. This is not just some trickle-down effect like the concept that even the dogs eat the scraps that fall from the master's table. It is not like saying that some children, though without a real relationship with God are still blessed by virtue of dwelling in a Christian home – No, this is bona fide blessing – that God actually favors certain people because of his love for someone else.

The second principle we learn from Peter directly regards the act of baptism. Peter, after the congregation is met with a sense of guilt for crucifying the Lord Christ and asks what they can do about it, tells them, "Repent, and let *every one of you* be baptized…" The act of baptism is significant, make no mistake, but the act of baptism was nothing new. What was revolutionary was the idea that *every one of them* could receive the baptism. This temple ritual, this ceremonial washing generally reserved for the priests, was now being offered to the commoners, to the laymen. Baptism had become a ritual applicable to *all* the repentant house of God. In this resides the uniqueness of the new covenant. Under the age of Christ, God's people have direct access to him through the Mediator – *all* God's people. There is none who are excluded from the ritual, for the ritual is a sign of inclusion, not exclusion. We call this the priesthood of believers. It is what Peter referred to in his epistle when he wrote, "Coming to Him as to a living stone, rejected indeed by men, but chosen by God and precious, you also, as living stones, are being built up a spiritual house, a holy priesthood, to offer up spiritual sacrifices acceptable to God through Jesus Christ." (1 Pet. 2.4-5) Peter refers to the church as a house, a temple, a priesthood. Every one of us has access to the most holy of places, for we *are* the temple of God through the mediation of Christ – we *are* the temple and we *are* made clean. Therefore the second principle that we learn is that baptism is an inclusive ordinance. It builds up. It does not tear down. It unites. It never divides.

With that being said, there is at least one more lesson to be learned from Peter's exposition regarding the Davidic Covenant – that children are included in it. Peter says, "Repent, and let every one of you be baptized...For the promise is for you and your children, and to all who are afar off, as many as the Lord our God will call." Now, this is where the water becomes so murky that the Baptists and the sacramentalists fail to see each other through it, so they choose to swim across to meet each other. The problem is that overlooking such disagreements does not result in real unity; it only results in the treading of water in the middle of murkiness. If it is unity we desire, then we must press on until it is unity that we have. Peter says the promise is for believers and their children, even for those who are far off, as many as God will call.

The first point of contention has to do with the promise in question. What is this promise to which Peter alludes – the promise that is for "you and your children?" Some might say that the promise is the promise of salvation. In that case, the promise is contingent upon repentance which is contingent upon being called. In other words, those who are called unto salvation are given the gift of repentance, and once repentance is exercised, then they may receive baptism. This is more or less the baptistic position. Children are included so long as they are able to repent and have been called by God, and the only way to know if they have been called by God is if repentance has been evidenced in their lives. Is this what the text indicates? Is this what Peter is teaching? Is Peter telling the congregation that their children are excluded from the house of Israel unless they have the ability to repent and exercise repentance? Is Peter really intending, upon this historic occasion, to reconstruct the understanding within the house of God as to the proper standing of their children? Is he really taking this opportunity to inform them that even though their children, from the beginning, have been granted a rightful inheritance within the covenant people, that in God's fulfillment of his redemptive plan and upon the outpouring of the Holy Spirit upon the Day of Pentecost, that that very standing has been removed? Is Peter really taking the time to preach an inclusive gospel only to place exclusive restrictions upon the house of Israel? Does Peter really make mention of children only to assume their exclusion from the very covenant he was so carefully expounding?

  Others say the promise is the Abrahamic covenant, the promise made to Abraham that God would make him the father of many nations and give him the land as an inheritance for his descendants. This is closer to the truth, but far too simplistic. The Davidic Covenant is in view here, not the Abrahamic, even though God's promise to David is certainly compatible, even an extension of his covenant with Abraham. It is easy to lump all promises together under one covenant, and ultimately that might make sense, but in particular cases and for particular situations, we should not be so sloppy as to assume that one round piece fits all round holes.

Yes, it is easy and it is tempting to make this mistake. If we could only make the connection between the promise to Abraham, whose children were partakers of that promise, and the words of Peter, then it would become clear that children are also partakers of the new covenant in Christ. Right? If only it was that easy, indeed.

But it need not be that easy. The words of Peter are clear. The promise of which Peter is referring is the Holy Spirit. We need not make an application that is not there, for the application is already made for us. "Repent, and let every one of you be baptized…and you *shall receive the gift of the Holy Spirit. For the promise is for you and your children…*" Peter prefaced these words by saying of Christ in his exposition of Psalm 16, "…And having received from the Father *the promise of the Holy Spirit*, He poured out this which you now see and hear." (Acts 2.33)

Being that the first point of contention concerns the identity of this promise, the second point of contention between the Baptists and the sacramentalists concerns the meaning of Peter's use of the word "call." The promise is for "as many as the Lord our God will call." The dissenters see this word "call" and immediately begin doing division. In so doing, the words "you", "children", and "all who are afar off", to convey any hope of the promise, are contingent upon being called. In that case, the first matter of business is to determine who is called. In order to determine this, they must be examined. If their lives and testimony are compatible with what is considered evident for someone who has been called, then, and only then is the promise said to be for them so that they may receive baptism. Again, this is a serious misrepresentation of Peter's proclamation. Peter is not doing systematic theology. He is not teaching the congregation about the ordo salutus. He is plainly preaching Christ. His use of the word "call" is not his starting point. It is his ending point. It is his conclusion. The promised Holy Spirit is for "you", "your children," and "all who are afar off." Peter is saying that these are the ones whom God calls. He is not making

God's call a mystery – no – he is explaining a mystery. He is saying, 'Do you wonder if you are called? Do you wonder if you have been made a part of God's house? Yes, you are a part! You, your children, and all who are afar off, as many as the Lord will call.' Peter is addressing those who are already a part of God's household. They need not enter in, for they are already there. Peter is simply telling them that it is Jesus, the one whom they crucified, who is both Lord and Christ. Therefore, repent and believe! Yes, salvation is dependent upon calling, but the point is that God is freely and actively engaged in the calling, right here and now. He is calling you, Oh Israel! He is calling your children! Yes, and he is even calling Gentiles – those who are afar off! Peter's point is that God is calling you! Why do we so easily take that to mean that God may *not* be calling you?

Let's sort this all out. First, God made a covenant with David that God would build a house for David and make his name great, even that there would be one who would come after him, one from his own body, whose throne would be established forever. "And your house and your kingdom shall be established forever before you. Your throne shall be established forever." Furthermore, even though it was not God's will that David himself would build a house for God, God did say that he who came after David would build "A house for My name, and I will establish the throne of his kingdom forever." David understood this promise to mean that he would live forever and that his kingdom would have no end. Furthermore, as Peter explains in his sermon, David understood that this promise would be fulfilled by the coming of a Christ, one who would come from his own body, one who would sit upon the throne forever, one who would be resurrected from the dead. This inspires David to write Psalm 16, which makes mention of David himself, that though he would die in the flesh, he would live vicariously through a Christ who would not see corruption, but instead would be raised from the dead so that in that way David would also be raised.

Peter indicates that this covenant which God made with David, this covenant which brought him to his knees in humble awe, was being fulfilled right before their very eyes in the pouring out of the Holy Spirit by the risen and exalted Christ. Peter is saying that the outpouring of the Spirit is the promise that was spoken to David – it is the construction phase of building "A house for My name." It was all coming to pass. The promise is, according to Peter, that through the pouring out of the Holy Spirit, God is building his church, and it is for you, your children, and all who are afar, even Gentiles, as many as God decides to call. Therefore, God is by no means excluding children from the covenant he makes with his people. More than including them in a covenant, he is including them in the church. God accepts children as members in his church. He receives children into the body of Christ. That is deduced from Peter's words concerning the promise that God made with David so long ago.

Now taking a step back for a moment before David, all the way back to the time of Abraham, we know that God made a covenant with Abraham which certainly included his children. All the males in his household were to be circumcised as a sign of God's grace and ownership over them. The Abrahamic covenant no doubt included children. Those who were born into the household of faith were required to bear the sign of redemption. With David, God is saying something even greater as it concerns our current dispensation. With David, God is saying that there will come a time when children are not only to be received into the covenant status but that they will be received into the body of Christ. They will receive the thing that was promised – namely, the Holy Spirit. To put it as plainly as I am able, the Holy Spirit's fulfillment of the Davidic covenant ensures that children of believers are full-fledged members of the Body of Christ. This time has come and now is.

18
MEDITATIONS ON CHILDREN AND SLAVES

***

Jesus said "Let the little children come to Me, and do not forbid them." (Matt. 19:4) Are these words not enough for us to understand that children are as equally accepted within the bosom of the church as anybody? Equality? Is that what this is about? No, it is not a matter of equality. Jesus does not consider children equal with adults. No, he places them so much higher. In fact, he makes them the prototype for his argument on humility. Jesus not only tells his disciples to stop hindering the children, but he says that "whoever does not receive the kingdom of God as a little child will by no means enter it." (Mark 10:15) Children, in Christ's mind, are the example of which we should strive. Maybe instead of prohibiting children from receiving baptism until they come of proper age and maturity, we should place the same prohibition upon adults. Maybe we should prohibit adult converts from receiving baptism until they become as naïve as a child. Ridiculous you say? Yes, ridiculous. I agree.

***

Jesus said, "Let the little children come to Me, and do not forbid them." Are these words so difficult to understand? If what Jesus meant by these words was to let the little children come to him and not to forbid them, then why are they being forbidden in at least half the churches in the world? Is baptism not coming to

Christ? These babes, these infants were not scooting themselves across the ground; they were not crawling to Christ in droves. The country side was not filled with crawling, rolling, and scooting babies, pouring out from the doorways of houses, lining the streets and the hillsides. No, they were not coming on their own volition. They were brought to Christ by their parents. They were brought to Christ so he could touch them. Just one touch. Just to see the hand of Christ upon the little sleeping heads, upon the little crying faces. The parents brought them because they knew there was something special, something sacred about this man Jesus. The parents brought them because they loved their babies. The parents brought them because the babies needed the Savior just as much as any of us do.

****

       Jesus said, "Let the little children come to Me, and do not forbid them , for such is the kingdom of God." (Mark 10.14-15) Yes, the kingdom of God belongs to such as children. Jesus wants each of us to come to him as a little child. If we do not, he says, we "will by no means enter it." Therefore, I think it would be prudent for us to study children. What are they like? How do they behave? This way we would know how we must become if we are to enter the kingdom of God. First, let us determine what children are *not.* They are not sinless and they are not always quiet. Therefore, we know that we are not required to be sinless and we must not always be quiet in order to enter the kingdom of God. That is refreshing to know. My sins and my annoying habits do not automatic disqualify me from being touched by the Savior. So what are babies like, then? They are helpless for sure. They are innocent in the ways of the world. They are absolutely dependent upon others, especially upon a mother. They need someone to feed them. They need someone to bathe them. They need someone to hold them. They are easily frightened, yet easily comforted. They are easily taken advantage of, even easily abused. But they are believers. They believe that at the breast they will be fed. They believe that at the outstretched arm they will be held. They smile at the sight of a familiar face. As they grow, they believe what they are told. They do not stop to reason. If they are told that stealing is wrong, then they will believe it. They will not always obey it, but they will believe it. If they are told from a young age that monkeys are hatched from the eggs of crocodiles, then they will believe it. They are eager to play, eager to please. Their imaginations are supreme, and consequently, their faith is too. They are imitators. They are followers. They are easily broken and easily mended. They are not skeptics. They are not cynical. They will leap from the roof top if you promise to catch them. They are oblivious, often times, of danger. In their infancy, they are the model of humility. Yes, humility. Is that what Jesus was saying, after all? Yes, of course! That is why the rich young ruler went away sad. (Matt. 19.22) It was because he refused to become like a little child. Yes, it is sad, but it is true – the older we get and the more of our childhood we leave behind, the less fit for the kingdom we actually become.

****

There is something that bothers me about all of this baby business. If we are to agree that this is what babies are like – and all it takes is a few moments of simple observation to determine it – then what are we to make of Jesus' statement that we must become like little children? How does that square with the practices in so many of our churches? Can we really become like little children while simultaneously excluding little children from our fellowship? Can we become like little children while at the same time forbidding little children to come and be touched and blessed by the Savior? Is that not what we teach in so many of our churches? Are we not teaching that we must take on the faith of a little child but exclude the child itself? It is a metaphor, we all agree. The child is a metaphor for what we must become if we are to enter the kingdom of God. But the thing that bothers me is this: why would Christ require us to become like the metaphor, but discard the metaphor itself? Why would Christ receive the adults who come to him as children but not receive the children who come to him as children? Is that not a preposterous notion? To receive the type while throwing away the prototype? But is that not what we are doing in so many of our churches? No, Jesus does no such thing. He receives the children first and then says that we must become like them.

****

But you, oh objector, I hear your cry! Your voice sounds mightily from the rooftop of the sanctuary, or the fellowship hall, or the multipurpose room, from wherever it is that you insist on keeping the children at arm's length. Your voice is loud and it is clear. Infants must not be baptized for they are incapable of faith! Repentance is impossible for them! Yes, I hear your cry, but there is one who cries louder than yourself. There is one whose cry reaches the ears of the Savior. There is the cry of the baby. Yes, the child can cry too, as we all know, and the Lord hears his cry. There is a story about Christ and how he entered Jerusalem on a donkey and how a great multitude laid clothes and tree branches across the road before him and worshipped, shouting "Hosanna to the Son of David!" (Matt. 21:1-17) Then Jesus went into the temple and overturned the money changers, driving out those who had turned his house into a "den of thieves." And upon this incident, something extraordinary happened. The blind and the lame came to him, and he healed them. And then the children began crying out in the temple. They, too, shouted, Hosanna to the Son of David!" In fact, their shouting was so mighty that the chief priests and the scribes could not help but take notice. They said to Jesus, "Do you hear what they are saying?" Oh foolish scribes! Oh priests, so unlearned! Have you no understanding? Have you no capacity for faith and repentance? Jesus heard, certainly he heard. He heard the cries of the children and he did not stop them. Instead, He said, "Have you not read, 'Out of the mouth of babes and nursing infants You have perfected praise?" Jesus turned to the psalmist to justify the cries of the children. For Jesus knew that just as he entered the city upon a lowly donkey, and just as he healed the blind and the lame, so also he received the praise from the mouths of the children. Yes, this is what the prophet Jeremiah must have understood when he used the phrase, "From the least of them to the greatest of them." (Jer. 31:34)

****

"Out of the mouth of babes and nursing infants You have perfected praise." The psalmist phrases it this way: "Out of the mouth of babes and nursing infants You have ordained strength." (Ps. 8:2) Why do we dare make such statements as we do about children? Why do we insist on presuming their idiocy in spiritual matters? Are we so much more capable than they? But they can't comprehend, we say. But who can comprehend spiritual things? Does not God's Word tell us that the carnal mind cannot understand God, (Rom. 8:7-8) that it is incapable of comprehension and dead in sin? So if spiritual understanding is not something which can be obtained through carnal maturity, through earthly education, why would we assume that children are incapable of such faith? Oh objector, have you not studied children? In what ways are they spiritually inferior to you? Their brains are not as mature, certainly, and they have not endured the practice of training their minds, nor have they lived long enough to gather a body of experience in the ways of the world, I will grant you. But will you hold that measure of innocence against them? Certainly they out-perform you in many other matters of faith. They will not dispute you when you instruct them in the sacraments. They will not differentiate between the bread and the body of Christ. No, you must teach them the difference, if there is such a difference. If you tell them, 'This is Christ's body,' they will believe it, for they have not yet learned how to become skeptics concerning the Word of God. Their minds have not yet matured to the point of doubt. If you tell them Jesus loves them and died for them, removing their sins from them, they will believe it and it will comfort them, even though they scarcely understand what death is. But all people, all those made in God's image, understand to some measure what sin is. And the child is honest. He will readily admit his guilt. He will not try to conceal the fact that he ate the cookies left out on the table. He will not clean up the crumbs in an attempt to conceal his guilt and escape punishment. No, deceit is something he must learn. It comes with practice and maturity of the mind. It comes by learning how to avert punishment – yes, that thing of which we adults have become so adept. Actually, it seems to me, just by using the reasoning capacity that I have developed over the years, be it however small, that although both children and adults are sinners, although both are selfish in their very nature, there is really only one major difference between children and adults when it comes to spiritual matters. Adults have become experts at hiding their deficiencies. Children have not. That does not make adults more spiritual; it only makes them more fraudulent. It seems to me that if it ever came down to a contest between the two, that it would be the child who would belong to the rite of baptism instead of the adult. Adults, just be thankful that God has not seen fit to have it come down to that.

"Out of the mouth of babes and nursing infants You have perfected praise." "Out of the mouth of babes and nursing infants You have ordained strength." There is an important lesson here that we are supposed to grasp. Children are among the physically weaker class of people. That is why they are mentioned along with the blind and the lame. But we tend to forget that these are those whom God seeks. That is why Jesus said that in order to enter his kingdom, we must first become like a little child. We must become as though we are blind. We must become lame. If our right eye causes us to stumble we must pluck it out. (Matt. 5.29) We must, in some measure, spiritually, maim ourselves. It is not proper to attempt to enter the kingdom of God as a rich man, as the young ruler sadly found out. It is not proper to attempt to enter the kingdom of God as a proud man as the Pharisees were constantly reminded. It is not proper to attempt to enter the kingdom of God as a whole man, as suffering teaches us. We are to be poor. We are to be humble. We are to be broken. The first will be last and the last will be first. (Matt. 20.16) If we want to be great in the kingdom of God, we must first become a servant. (Matt. 23.11) Yes, a slave. We must become slaves of Christ. Over and over again we are taught this by the Savior, yet when it comes to baptizing children, we fail to grasp the concept. What is it about the water that is too holy for them? What is it about the ceremony that is too sacred? Why are we keeping the children away from the water? Do they not believe? Are we not teaching our children to believe? Ultimately, the water is Christ. It is the work of the Holy Spirit in bringing us to Christ. I think it should be quite clear that Christ does not want us to prevent our children from coming to him. That we should understand at the very minimum. But in these words of Jesus and in the words of the psalmist, there is something even more striking, something even more simple. It is the fact that children really can have faith. It is the fact that children really can praise God – and not just children, but nursing infants. Who are we to presume to know the mind of the babe? Who are we to presume to judge the faith of the infant? Christ is teaching us that faith is a gift of God. It is God who perfects praise. The psalmist is teaching us that strength comes from God. It is God who ordains strength. It is God who uses the foolish things of the world to shame the wise, the weak things of the world to upset the strong. (1 Cor. 1:27) The issue of baptism is not whether children have the capacity for faith and repentance, or whether they have all the catechism questions memorized, or whether they have prayed an adequate prayer. The issue of baptism is whether or not they belong to God. Does God receive them as his own? Does God perfect their praise?

****

Jesus said, "Whoever receives one little child like this in My name receives Me. Whoever causes one of these little ones who believes in Me to sin, it would be better for him if a millstone were hung around his neck, and he were drowned in the depths of the sea." (Matt. 18:5-6) Apparently, Jesus thought little children could have faith. Apparently, Jesus also thought that it was important to receive the children in his name. In fact, it was so important that not doing so brings the threat of destruction. Consider Christ's words. Whoever causes the child to sin…Whoever causes the child to stumble… Let the children come and forbid them not… What is the greater sin? Allowing children to be baptized? Or keeping them away from Christ? What do you think Jesus would say about that? God forbid we push our children away so often that they begin to lose interest. Does that ever happen in our churches? I am not sure there are enough millstones to go around.

****

There is this business of household baptisms to contend with. At least three times in the New Testament Scriptures are we given an account of an entire household being baptized after the conversion of one of the household members. (1) How are we to reconcile the concept of household baptisms with the baptistic understanding that baptism is contingent upon an adequate profession of faith and repentance? Ah, that is easy, the dissenters say. There is no proof that there were children or infants in those households. Therefore, we must assume that all members of the household were of proper age and maturity. Yes, that is true. There is no proof of such a thing. But neither is their proof that there was not. There is still a problem, and that is the fact that there were household baptisms. The problem lies in the continuity between the Old Testament practice and the New Testament practice. Even though these are Gentile believers being baptized, the old covenant practice of household inclusion remains intact. Certainly the mention of household baptisms is no proof of the legitimacy of infant baptisms, but it is proof of one thing. It is proof that even in the New Testament era, God looks upon households in the same way he looked upon them when he made his covenant with Abraham. God still looks upon households as a community of faith.

****

If there are those who consider it wrong to assume that children are members of Christ's body, the Apostle Paul is not among them. In his letter to the Ephesians, he takes great care to demonstrate the nature of the church, and in doing so, upholds the case for children as members of the church. Sure, it is not anywhere near his purpose for writing the letter, and it does not come boldly glaring off the pages of Scripture, but it is there nonetheless. It is there latent, as if the apostle takes it for granted. He writes as though everyone in the world already knew that children were part of the church. He does the same thing in his letter to the Colossians. He is assuming that children would be present in the reading of the letter. He is assuming that the congregation has already understood, even as Gentiles, the principles of covenant community.

****

Consider the language that is used throughout the letter to the Ephesians. "He has blessed *us* with every spiritual blessing…Just as He chose *us* in Him…having predestined *us* to adoption as sons…" (Eph. 1.3-5) Who are the "us" of whom he refers? Well, Paul of course, and everyone to whom he is addressing the letter, namely the saints in Ephesus, or the church body which resides there. Notice that Paul does not differentiate between classes of Christians. Notice he does not attempt to drive a wedge between those who believe and those who are only pretending. There is no wedge driving taking place. There is only the assumption of unity and singularity. There is the assumption of oneness. "In Him you also trusted…in whom also, having believed, you were sealed with the Holy Spirit of promise…" (Eph. 1.13) Again, no division when he addresses the church. And remember the Holy Spirit of promise? What was the promise but the building of the church? Remember how that promise includes children? Paul understands that perfectly. In fact, he identifies Christ's church as that "which is His body, the fullness of Him who fills all in all." (Eph. 1.22-23) Later, Paul refers to the church as a holy temple. Remember the House for My name? He refers to Christ as being the chief cornerstone, "in whom the whole building, being fitted together, grows into a holy temple in the Lord, in whom you are also being built together for a dwelling place of God in the Spirit." (Eph. 2.21) Who is Paul addressing? Is it adults only? Is it adults only who have made proper profession of faith and have shown an acceptable measure of repentance? Or is it the entire assembly? Read these words carefully. Read the entire letter carefully. Read it in one sitting. Read it as a letter of exhortation. Then tell me whether children are excluded from the assembly. Then tell me whether the principles of the old covenant have been broken under the New Testament teaching.

Paul writes concerning the church, "...grow up in all things into Him who is the head – Christ – from whom the whole body, joined and knit together by what every joint supplies, according to the effective working by which every part does its share, causes growth of the body for the edifying of itself in love." (Eph. 4:15-16) Are not children part of this exhortation? Are they not part of the "whole body, joined and knit together?" Do they not also share in the "growth of the body for the edifying of itself in love?" It seems that Jesus thought so. It is quite evident that Paul thought so as well, even as he encourages the Ephesians to "be imitators of God as dear children." (Eph. 5:1) Certainly these words are meant to bring unity between Jew and Gentile, but are not children joined and knit together as well? And what about slaves? Do they have a part in the body of Christ?

Of course children are members of the church! For Paul admits, when discussing the family, that "we are members of His body, of His flesh and of His bones." (Eph. 5:30) The family, says the apostle, is the outworking of the church. It is the expression of the covenant bond between Christ and the redeemed. The family has not been broken by God. Rather, God upholds the family as a community of faith. God certainly does not want the family to become an idol, nor does he want it to become a hindrance in our walk with him, that is evident when Christ said we must hate our family if we are to follow him. (Luke 14.26) But the radical repentance required by Christ does not interrupt the favor that God shows entire households, nor does it exclude children from partaking in the grace that is offered in the church. That is why Paul specifically addresses children in his letter. After stressing the whole body, joined and knit together, and after admitting that the marriage covenant demonstrates that we are members of Christ's body, Paul immediately addresses children. He says, "Children, obey your parents in the Lord, for this is right." (Eph. 6.1) In his letter to the Colossians, Paul writes, "Children, obey your parents in all things, for this is well pleasing to the Lord." (Col. 3.20) In Romans, Paul stated that "Those who are in the flesh cannot please God." (Rom. 8.8) Here, in Colossians, Paul explains that children, in obedience to their parents, *are* able to please the Lord. Therefore, Paul must not assume that children are in the flesh. No, I think he assumes that they are in the Lord.

****

"Children, obey your parents in all things, for this is well pleasing to the Lord." Most Christian parents and most churches love Scripture like this because it is readily accessible every time our children do wrong. If our children fail to feed the dog after we tell them to feed the dog, then we have this verse at our fingertips. But the irony is that in many of our homes and in many of our churches we only use this admonishment as it is convenient to us without regard to what it really means. If we are to hold our children to obedience on account of this verse in Colossians, then we are really holding them to something much more than we may even realize. We are holding them to covenant obligations. We are saying, without even realizing it much of the time, that our children belong to the Lord. We are calling upon their responsibility as members of the church, as citizens of the kingdom of God. Do we really believe this to be the case? If so, why do they not receive baptism? If not, why do we expect them to act as if they belonged? In the latter case, we should not admonish them but plead for them.

★★

But there is something else amazing in what Paul writes to the Colossians. He refers to them as the elect. He says, "Therefore, as the elect of God…" (Col. 3:12) Then he speaks to the children. He speaks to the wives. He speaks to the husbands. He speaks to the fathers. And he speaks to the children. He speaks to them as "the elect of God." Why would he call them elect if they are not considered members in the church? Yes, and then he speaks to the bondservants.

★★

"Bondservants, obey in all things your masters according to the flesh, not with eyeservice as men-pleasers, but in sincerity of heart, fearing God." (Col. 3:22) Is it not curious that slaves were mentioned among the family members? Is it not also curious that slaves were mentioned among the church? And not only are they mentioned, but they are told "whatever you do, do it heartily, as to the Lord and not to men, knowing that from the Lord you will receive the reward of the inheritance, for you serve the Lord Christ." (Col. 3:23-24) There were obviously slaves, or bondservants, in the midst of the Colossians, and they were counted among the assembly. They also were included in the whole body with those who were joined and knit together. They were counted among the elect. They were counted among those who were chosen and predestined. They were counted among the "us" and the "you" of whom Paul refers. Certainly, they must have been baptized, were they not? And certainly they would have been considered no higher than the children of the house, would they? Certainly, if we were to drive a wedge in the congregation (something we wish not to do, nor does Paul) then we would drive it between those who are free and those who are in bondage, would we not? The conclusion is clear, simple really. Not only are the children of the church no less members of the church than the most articulate preacher, they are no less members than the lowest slave. Certainly, they are no less sinners. Certainly, they are no less believers. Then why in Christ's name do we insist on keeping them away from the waters of baptism? Will it kill them to get a little wet? No, it will not kill them, but it just might save them no less.

19
THE CASE FOR INFANT BAPTISM

The case for including infants in the cleansing ritual of baptism has been addressed quite thoroughly over the centuries by a number of Biblical scholars; a concise, pointed, and passionate plea can be found in Charles Hodge's Systematic Theology, (1) so it is not my intention here to reinvent the baptismal font, but only to remind ourselves of the logic of the argument as a further springboard for this particular discourse. The syllogism goes something like this:

1. Circumcision was the sign of the gospel, or covenant inclusion, for God's people in the Old Testament era.
2. Children were included, or counted among, God's people in the Old Testament era.
3. Therefore, children received the sign of the gospel, or covenant inclusion, in the Old Testament era.
4. Baptism is the sign of the gospel, or covenant inclusion, for God's people in the New Testament era.
5. At no time has God excluded children from being counted among God's people in the New Testament era.
6. Therefore, children should receive the sign of the gospel (baptism) in the New Testament era.

Concerning the first point, I have no knowledge that it is anywhere in dispute that circumcision was the covenant sign for God's people in the days before Christ. Israel was God's chosen nation established through the patriarchs, beginning with Abraham. When God came to the childless Abraham promising him that he would become the father of many nations and that his children would inherit the land of Canaan, God required circumcision as a sign unto that covenant, or, as we addressed previously, a seal unto God's righteousness. This sign was to be applied to all males within his household – not only his own offspring, but any males obtained by purchase. These persons, these circumcised males of Abraham's household, were counted among God's people. We know this because the promise is not without a warning. God says that if any are to go without the sign that he will cut them off from among the people, for that would be a violation of the covenant. (Gen. Ch. 17)

Concerning the second point, it is quite obvious that the children of the Israelites were no less privileged to be counted among God's people as were their parents. This is evident, firstly, in the promise itself when God says, "This is My covenant which you shall keep, between Me and you and *your descendants after you.*" (Gen. 17:10) But furthermore, God everywhere throughout the testimony of Israel considers the children to be full citizens of Israel and beneficiaries of the covenant made with Abraham. This is the God who described himself as "...A jealous God, visiting the iniquity of the fathers upon the children to the third and fourth generations of those who hate Me, but showing mercy to thousands, to those who love Me and keep My commandments." (Ex. 20:5-6) This is the God who, infuriated by the Israelites after they unconscionably slaughtered and sacrificed their own children, called them his own by saying, "Moreover you took your sons and your daughters, whom you bore to Me, and these you sacrificed to them to be devoured. Were your acts of harlotry a small matter, that you have slain My children and offered them up to them by causing them to pass through the fire?" (Ez. 16:20-21) This is the God who "seeks godly offspring" (Mal 2:15) according to the prophet Malachi. Yes, this is the God of Joshua, who, when confronted with the choice of following the pagan tendencies of the Israelites or remaining faithful to the Lord, said, "Choose for yourselves this day whom you will serve...But for me and my house, we will serve the Lord." (Josh. 24:15) The pages of the Old Testament Scriptures are filled with references concerning the Israelite children, integrating the children into the lifeblood of the covenant, and in every case God is calling them his own. Never is there a hint of exclusion. Never is there a hint of omission. Never is there a hint of the need to enter in. They are already in. They are members of the House of Israel.

This leads us to the next point. This sign, this covenant of circumcision, was to be applied to children – yes, even infants. In fact, newborn males were to receive the sign upon the eighth day after their birth. God required this bloody mark to be borne upon the flesh of his people as a sign of the covenant between himself and Abraham. That the children of Israel were required to comply with this procedure is nowhere in dispute. It is the sign which set them apart from the other nations. It identified them as God's chosen people, and furthermore, any outsider who desired to take Israel's God as his own and participate in the Passover meal, for instance, was required to comply. It was essential to being called a child of Abraham. Even more importantly, it was essential to being called a child of God.

The fourth point has been beaten to death in the first two parts of this book, and if the point that baptism is a sign and seal of the gospel of grace under the church age has not been driven home, then I have failed tragically within these pages. The fact is that just as circumcision was the covenant sign for God's people before the coming of Christ, so baptism is the covenant sign for God's people henceforth the coming of Christ. God has not placed a moratorium upon covenant signs. God has not ceased to be a covenant making God. Remember, the nature of the covenant has not changed; only its form has changed. Baptism in the New Testament era is a sign of the gospel. This is evident by Jesus' words, "Go therefore and make disciples of all the nations, baptizing them in the name of the Father and of the Son and of the Holy Spirit."

It is upon the fifth point that the controversy begins to arise. But there is a critical notation to be made first. It is admitted that this logic only works under the assumption that the church is the new Israel, as we are taught in Galatians 6:16. If we maintain the opinion that all of these covenant promises and requirements that are manifested throughout the Old Testament Scriptures are unique only to a particular people, only applicable to a certain body politic, then we may have a problem grasping the concept of a 'new Israel'. If we insist that the concept of Israel is distinct from the concept of a church body, then we may not be able to choke down the reasoning of the syllogism. But if we dare to acknowledge, like the pages of the New Testament seem to indicate and the words of Peter seem to scream, that there is now no difference between Jew and Gentile, (Rom. 10:12) that the wall of separation has been destroyed, (Eph. 2:14) that the covenant that God made with Abraham and the one he made with David are still intact, and that Christ did not come to abolish the law and the prophets, but to fulfill them, (Matt. 5:17) then all this chatter about continuity between the Old and New Testaments becomes much easier to digest. The truth is that the New Testament church is the fulfillment of the Old Testament shadow that was the nation of Israel. Though political, it was always spiritual. God's people are God's people. He has only one people. It is made up of Jews and Gentiles who confess Christ as Lord.

I have diverted here from my proper topic of discourse, but it must be mentioned as a precursor to understanding the proper nature of baptism. For if God entertains two distinct peoples, if God maintains a double standard for salvation, then the above reasoning falls apart, for in that case all the covenant laws, rituals, and promises that were entrusted to Israel may be kept with Israel as a body politic, and all the New Testament instruction may be applied specifically to the Gentile believers. This would certainly disrupt the balance and continuity between the Old Testament sign of circumcision and the New Testament sign of baptism, I admit. But we need not concern ourselves with that. The pretended division between God's Old Testament people and his New Testament people is so contrived, so full of hoops and tight ropes, that an exegetical circus is needed to entertain it, for the New Testament writers everywhere draw upon God's covenant with Abraham as the foundation upon which the New Testament church stands.

But moving on to the fifth point is where the controversy really begins to surface. For even if you accept the assumption that there is continuity between Israel and the church, you are not necessarily forced to accept the idea that at no time has God excluded children from being counted among God's people in the New Testament era. There are many who will wholeheartedly accept the overarching premise of covenant continuity and still reject this concept of child inclusion on exegetical grounds. They would argue, "No, as a matter of fact, God *does* exclude children from his covenant under the church age unless they come to Christ in a Biblically prescribed manner – namely faith and a repentance that can be verified through experience and observation."

In other words, although circumcision was the covenant sign for God's people in the Old Testament, and although children were included among God's covenant people in the Old Testament and therefore bore the sign of circumcision, and although the covenant sign has been changed to baptism under the New Testament era, children are no longer given the sign because they are no longer automatically considered covenant members. Therefore, if this is true, then something has obviously changed. At some point between the coming of Christ and the organization of the New Testament church, children became excluded. Suddenly, the practice that the people of God had maintained for centuries, the concept that the children of the covenant were members of the covenant and that God considered them his own, has been altered. Suddenly, in the new and better covenant, in the era of fulfillment, in the coming of Christ – suddenly, children are excluded from the things of God. They have become the Gentiles of old.

The problem is that this abruption, this sudden halt, is not articulated in Scripture. It is not made plain. The lack of revelation in this matter is often referred to as the argument from silence. It is silence because the Scriptures are silent, and because of this it is an extremely loud silence indeed! The primary question being asked by believers in the New Testament was whether or not Gentiles could be part of the church. This is because the inclusion of Gentiles was a revolutionary concept to many of the Jews. Even though it was foreshadowed in the law and the prophets, the fact that God was reaching into the uttermost regions of the earth and engrafting outsiders was an earth shattering concept. It affected how they worshipped, what they ate, who they associated with, etc. The argument from silence asks simply this: if the likewise revolutionary concept of excluding children from covenant membership was suddenly the norm, then why was nobody talking about it? And why were there no controversies in the church regarding it?

This is the crux of the disunion between the inclusive crowd and the exclusive crowd and consequently the crux of the issue of infant baptism. Do children belong or not? Are they partakers of the covenant promises and included in the body of Christ by virtue of God's institution, or is their membership in the church contingent upon something in addition to a divine promise? We already know that children are included not only in the Abrahamic covenant but the Davidic covenant, and that the children of believers are partakers of the work that the Holy Spirit is doing to build Christ's church. But if that is true, then why is there such animosity towards infant baptism? Apart from the insistence on the division between Israel and the church, there is one primary reason for this animosity, as far as I can gather, and it has to do with a prophecy by Jeremiah which was reiterated by the writer of Hebrews.

20
CHILDREN OF THE NEW COVENANT

The Lord spoke through the prophet Jeremiah concerning the future when he said, "Behold, the days are coming when I will make a new covenant with the house of Israel and with the house of Judah." (Jer. 31:31) The writer to the Hebrews picks up on this promised new covenant in chapter eight and applies it to the church by writing, "If the first covenant had been faultless, then no place would have been sought for a second," and also, "In that He says, 'A new covenant,' He has made the first obsolete. Now what is becoming obsolete and growing old is ready to vanish away." (Heb. 8:7,13)

This concept of a new covenant is evidence of a few things. First, it is evidence that there is such a thing as an old covenant, or to put it another way, a first covenant. Therefore, there is a distinction in some measure between a prior covenant made by God and new covenant made by God. Secondly, it is evident that this new covenant replaces the old covenant as the standing and working relationship between God and his people. In addition, the concept of a new covenant is evidence that God has made something better. By calling the old covenant obsolete, he implies that the new covenant is an upgrade. So the first question might be: what exactly is this old covenant to which Jeremiah is referring?

He is referring to the covenant that God made with Israel – No, more so – It is the covenant that God made with Israel as it was applied through the Mosaic ordinances! The covenant which the writer called obsolete was the Mosaic covenant, the rites and rituals of the people of old, the shadows of the things to come. The covenant which the writer called obsolete was the covenant established through the sacrifice of bulls and goats, the covenant of an earthly high priest. This is the covenant that was passing away. It was *not* the covenant that God made with Abraham. It was *not* the covenant that God made with David. It was the covenant that God made with Moses *only in the practical expression of it*. This is plain. In this, there is no dispute. It is evident in two ways – first, in that this is the very theme of the Epistle to the Hebrews; it was written to uphold the Abrahamic covenant while proving that Christ is the fulfillment of the ordinances, that Christ, not the law, is the righteousness of Israel; but secondly, it is evident in the use of the language from the Abrahamic covenant which is reiterated throughout the law and the prophets, that language of "I will be your God," or "You shall be my people" or I will be a God to them." This is how God speaks about his chosen people. There is no change in this language as the covenant moves from the old to the new. In fact, there is no change in the nature of the covenant at all. The covenant is called new because it has been fulfilled by Christ. Christ has come and has made intercession. Christ has come and has made sacrifice. Christ has come and has been made the High Priest over the House of Israel. Christ has come – that is how the covenant has been made new. In that way, the regulations of the Mosaic covenant have been made obsolete even though the covenant itself has remained intact.

So this is the covenant to which Jeremiah and the writer of Hebrews refer. The question for our topic at hand is this: does the formation of a new covenant affect the children? Or, in other words, is God's announcement that he is making a new covenant and that the old is becoming obsolete to be understood that children should no longer receive the covenant sign of the gospel? The Baptist says yes, it does mean that! It means that children are no longer accepted into the community of God's people just by virtue of being born into the midst of God's people! The Baptist says that children are born outside the circle, outside the community, and must be brought in the same way any pagan must be brought in – by faith and repentance. In fact, the Baptist would say (maybe not across the board, but certainly many) that there is no longer a covenant which assumes any particular people; rather that the covenant that was once overarching, that was once identifiable by the community it incorporated, is now obsolete, passing with the formation of the new covenant – that the new covenant is not incorporated at all, but rather, internal, subjective, isolated, and/or individual. They talk and act as if the only covenant which really matters is the one that God makes with each person individually, and he does that by an internal calling only, a mysterious work of the Holy Spirit unverifiable by outside sources except to wait and watch and determine whether the individual produces the adequate amount of fruit and repentance.

Is this what is meant by the new covenant? Has it really become a covenant not only between God and Abraham, but between God and Billy, God and Jerry, God and Steve, God and Sally? Is it no longer a covenant between God and Israel? Is it no longer a covenant between God and believers, along with their households? How new is the new covenant? How different is it from the old? Is it really true that God no longer favors communities or households or even nations? Does God only keep his eye upon the individual soul? Let's take a closer look at the prophecy from Jeremiah:

> *"Behold, the days are coming, says the LORD, when I will make a new covenant with the house of Israel and with the house of Judah – not according to the covenant that I made with their fathers in the day that I took them by the hand to lead them out of the land of Egypt, My covenant which they broke, though I was a husband to them, says the LORD. But this is the covenant that I will make with the house of Israel*

> *after those days, says the LORD: I will put My law in their minds, and write it on their hearts; and I will be their God, and they shall be My people. No more shall every man teach his neighbor, and every man his brother, saying, 'Know the LORD,' for they all shall know Me, from the least of them to the greatest of them, says the LORD. For I will forgive their iniquity, and their sin I will remember no more."* (Jer. 31:31-34)

This is the Old Testament prophecy which the New Testament writer of Hebrews applied to his current circumstances under the age of Christ, and this is the prophecy which the baptistic minded folks understand to mean that under the age of Christ the covenant has become predominantly subjective and exclusive. Is this what the writer of Hebrews intended?

To the Baptists, the key element of this prophecy is that portion which seems to emphasize the subjective, or internal, aspects of the covenant. God will make a *new* covenant, he says. In it, he will put his laws upon his peoples' minds and he will write them on their hearts. This might be understood to mean that outward forms of the covenant are done away with, that under the new covenant God deals with man on a more internal basis. In other words, those whom God covenants with will receive his laws upon their minds and hearts. Those whom God excludes will not. Furthermore, no longer will a man teach his neighbor saying 'Know the Lord,' for they will all know me. The Baptists understand this to mean that under the new covenant, all the members of that covenant will know the Lord intimately. Or, to put it more accurately under this interpretation, under the new covenant, the only ones who should be considered members of the covenant are those who know God intimately. If you are regenerate, you are a covenant member. If you are not, then you are not a covenant member, even if you are baptized, even if you partake in church life, even if you are born into a Christian household. Unless you know God personally, meaning that unless you have confessed your sins and show that you have placed your faith in Christ, you are an outsider. That is what Baptists believe. That, as you can plainly determine, is contrary to the culture of the Old Testament. It is repulsed by the old notion of inclusivity in Israel. That is why they exclude children from the covenant community. That is why even though children were included in the Abrahamic covenant, even though children were included in the Davidic covenant, even though Peter included them in his sermon on the Holy Spirit and the church, even though Jesus brought them near and specifically said that the kingdom of Heaven belongs to those like them, even though God calls them his own over and over and over again, and even though they are addressed as members of the church in the epistles, certainly they are not members of the covenant because Jeremiah said that new covenant members are only those who "Know the Lord."

The problem is that Jeremiah does *not* say that. Neither does the writer to the Hebrews. Neither does God. It is not safe to assume that by "Know the Lord," he is implying some sort of internal faith connection. Rather, when taken within the context of the overarching theme of Hebrews, "Know the Lord" means Christ is High Priest as is evidenced in the verse which immediately precedes the above passage, a verse which reads, "But now He has obtained a more excellent ministry, inasmuch as He is now Mediator of a better covenant, which was established on better promises." (Heb. 8:6)

The whole point of the new covenant is that it is better than the old one on the basis of the finished work of Christ. In that sense, God's laws are written upon our minds and hearts. In that sense we will all "Know the Lord." We will all know him because we can come to him directly. We no longer need the mediation of an earthly priest when we can petition the Heavenly One. To take this prophecy and narrow it is a travesty against the spirit of the prophecy. To take this prophecy and minimize it in no way makes it better. This is a better covenant. It is not a different covenant. It is better. Taking a system that has included children and suddenly excluding them does not make the system better. Taking an expansive grace and narrowing it to the point of subjectivity does not make the grace better. It only makes it smaller. Under the New Testament, every indication is that the kingdom is bigger, not smaller. The mustard seed grows. It doesn't shrivel up. The dough rises. It doesn't go flat. Yes, it is important to know the Lord. It is crucial to trust Christ for your salvation. Your life depends upon it. But to say that we should exclude certain people whom God has included just because their faith is not as mature as someone older is to deflate the kingdom of God and water down the blood of Christ.

    But there are other problems as well. There is the fact that Jeremiah was addressing this prophesy to the house of Israel. God says that the days are coming when he will make a new covenant *with the house of Israel.* The writer of Hebrews makes no exception. He acknowledges that the prophecy was for the house of Israel. Then why does he apply it to the church? Because the church *is* the house of Israel. The church is the house of Israel under the new covenant. This is the thing that God foretold to David which brought him to his knees, and this is what Peter was telling the congregation who were cut to the heart. God is not making a different covenant. He is applying the covenant of old to the church, to the new man, to Jew and Gentile alike, and he is fulfilling it and making it better through the redemption and righteousness that is found in his Son. It is like when you buy a new computer or a new car. You might very well buy the same exact model, only with upgrades. That is the new covenant. It is the same model with upgrades. The carnality of the symbols and foreshadows have passed. The spirituality of the fulfillment in Christ has come. Baptism, as the new covenant sign of the gospel, has replaced circumcision, the old covenant sign of the gospel, because it is a better sign. God is not in the business of reduction, but multiplication.

If we admit that the promise of the new covenant is for the church, then we have already conceded the biggest point of contention to infant baptism – the insistence on the distinction between Israel and the church. If we admit that this promise is a better covenant because it is more expansive, then we have conceded the second biggest point of contention to infant baptism – the insistence on the subjectivity of the covenant. There is no room in this promise to shrink the covenant. Given that the context is compatible with the old mantra of "I will be their God, and they will be My people," and given that it is addressed to the house of Israel, there is no room to interpret this Scripture the way the Baptists want to interpret it, namely that the members of the church are only those who have been subjectively regenerated. If we were to shrink the concept of the church so greatly and use the phrase "They will all know me" in the way that the Baptists do, then we must conclude that there is either really no such thing as a covenant community or that the entire house of Israel, the entire church, will know Christ savingly, including children and hypocrites. If the promise is "They will all know Me," and if the context is the covenant community at large, then the conclusion must be that either a covenant community does not exist or that the covenant community will all be saved. Does not the baptistic understanding of Hebrews eight tend to bite the hand which feeds it? It seems so to me.

There is continuity here, certainly, between the old covenant and the new, and there is one more nugget of continuity that I have yet to mention. There is the often used phrase, "From the least of them to the greatest of them." Now admittedly, this phrase is not always a direct reference to children, but it is certainly not exclusive of children. Children are considered, normally, under the category of "least of them." There are others too. There are slaves and cripples, poor and unclean, and children. Basically, this phrase, used over and over again in Scripture, refers to the lowest social classes. Even they, God is saying, will know me. Again, that is not implying that all of them without exception will be saved, but rather, it is asserting that all of them without exception have access to Christ through his work of mediation within the covenant. They would have to be covenant members to have that kind of access. No one disputes the fact that a blind man may be baptized, but it seems that the blind man's newborn daughter is to be left in the gutter until she matures to a proper age.

Finally, in conclusion of this chapter, let me leave you to consider some further words, with a similar tone, as recorded by the prophet Jeremiah. Note the connection between the words 'children' and 'everlasting': "They shall be my people and I shall be their God, then I will give them one heart and one way, that they may fear Me forever, for the good of them *and their children after them.* And I will make an everlasting covenant with them..." (Jer. 32:38-40)

Is this so different from the other context we've been dealing with? Yet here, children are expressly mentioned.

21
PILGRIM'S PROGRESS THEOLOGY

Every once in a while a book is written which alters the landscape of a culture. Such is the case in the United States with the 1852 publishing of Uncle Tom's Cabin by Harriet Beecher Stowe. Books can sometimes do that. It is possible that they take on a life of their own, personifying even beyond the influence of their authors. It was not Stowe who people looked to. It was the book entitled Uncle Tom's Cabin. It was the book that became bedrock of abolitionist sentiments. It was Uncle Tom, not Stowe, who became the good natured, long suffering martyr.

What Uncle Tom's Cabin was able to do for the 19th century western political world, The Pilgrim's Progress by John Bunyan was able to do for the theological world ever since its publication in the late 17th century. Just as Uncle Tom has become an icon for victimization, Christian, the hero of The Pilgrim's Progress, has become an icon for the normal Christian life. He, in a way, has become an icon for salvation.

The Pilgrim's Progress maintains its place atop a pedestal in literature mainly because of its profound influence, and it certainly is profound in many aspects. The allegorical characters which come and go along the pilgrim journey truly depict the broad variance of experiences any Christian encounters in his pursuit of eternal life. Places such as Vanity Fair or the Doubting Castle, people such as the subtle Talkative or the stubborn Ignorance. These are places we have all been. These are people we have all known. We may even wonder if they are actually ourselves. The Pilgrim's Progress expertly reveals the snares and pitfalls of the Christian life lived in pursuit of holiness. It is not always obvious.

It is rarely easy. It requires help, for it is impossible of our own accord.

Yet for all the truth depicted within the pages of The Pilgrim's Progress, there are other things not quite right, things amiss, aberrations equally as profound as the truths. Pardon me for saying so, but although The Pilgrim's Progress is a bastion of sound doctrine, so is it also a slough of misconceptions.

To be fair, it is a slough of one particular misconception which leads into the application of further misconceptions. The Pilgrim's Progress is about salvation. It is about the pursuit of eternal life. Even more particularly, I think, it is about conversion. And that is the problem – not that it depicts conversion per se – but what it implies about conversion. The story depicts Christian's conversion as being primarily inward and individual. But conversion *is* internal, you say! It is the inward change that is the result of the Holy Spirit bringing me from death to life! Is that all it is? If you think so, thank The Pilgrim's Progress for that. Even if you have never read it, thank The Pilgrim's Progress for that.

The story is really not a story at all. It is a catechism with characters. It is great, mind you. It is sometimes silly, but sometimes powerful – even convicting – and for that it serves the author's purpose superbly. The problem is that it promotes a baptistic perspective of the road to eternal life. It assumes a purely inward conception of conversion. Just as John Bunyan was a Baptist (though charitable to the opposite opinion), so is The Pilgrim's Progress an excellent example of baptistic thought. The manner in which this is demonstrated is that the story isolates the doctrine of salvation from the other essential categories of theology, namely ecclesiology and eschatology.

One reason for the lack of unity within the church in the area of baptism is a result of the lack of unity in the areas of ecclesiology and eschatology. In fact, baptism can never be debated effectively if these other categories are ignored because one's understanding of baptism will inevitably be determined by one's understanding of the church and the eternal kingdom. When we attempt to separate salvation from the church and the eternal kingdom, we begin to slip into a casual understanding of the latter two. We begin to push them out toward the margins of central doctrines. When this happens, baptistic theology results.

I am not saying that The Pilgrim's Progress is responsible for divorcing salvation from the church and the eternal kingdom, but it has certainly validated the divorce maybe more than any other single piece of literature in history. It tells the story of Christian, laden with a burden upon his back, who believes the threats and promises of the book which he has been given, so he sets out upon a journey to find the Celestial City in which he has come to believe. But he knows not how to get there. Therefore, he is dependent upon the help of others who interpret the book for him and point him in the right direction. Along the way, he encounters many characters, some genuine, but most deceptive and bent on either destruction or pretention. However, by continuing on the narrow path, Christian is loosed from his burden and eventually crosses the river into the Celestial City. The allegory is meant to show how an individual is brought from destruction to life, from infancy to maturity. The problem is that he does this without the church, and frankly, without any clear evidence of baptism.

Sure, he has friends. He has companionship from time to time. Faithful and Hopeful are his best friends. He benefits from conversing with them. They edify him and he them. But they do not worship together. They do not really do anything together except talk together along the journey. In fact, when Christian defeats Apollyon , he is alone. When Christian travels through the Valley of the Shadow of Death, he is alone. Even when he crosses the river into the Celestial Kingdom, although Hopeful goes with him, he crosses alone. When he partakes of the bread and the wine, he does so alone. It is true that for ourselves – in that place where we are confronted with eternity, in that moment of self-examination when we become conscious of our eternal destiny – it is true there and then that we are ultimately alone with God, for if we are to be saved, then we must be saved alone. Yet we are not alone! Though our eternal destiny is set for ourselves and ourselves alone, we do not travel alone. A covenant making God covenants not with us alone, but with all his people collectively. The Pilgrim's Progress, as an allegory, leaves no room for the collective Christian experience. The story leaves no room for the church, for Christian worship, for corporate prayer, for baptism and the Lord's Supper, for the preached Word. No, everything that is done is done individually. He believes alone. He wrestles alone. He struggles alone. He goes alone.

Yes, he goes alone. Why is Christian never baptized? Why is he never brought into the company of saints until he arrives at his final destination? Was the river his baptism? If so, why does it take place so long after he is identified as a Christian? No, I think the river, if it is a baptism, is a baptism into death, as it seems to represent his entrance into a place called Heaven. Should we assume that Christian was baptized sometime before the story begins? There is certainly no indication of this. But as curious as it is that there is no legitimate representation of baptism in the progress of our pilgrim, it is even more curious how easily he leaves his wife and children to the freedom of their own wills. Yes, in this way, Christian goes alone.

Sure, he wishes they would come with him, his dear wife and his little babes. He even admits to having pleaded with them. Oh, he is quick to admit that much, even to the point of whining about it, as if intruding into the freedom of their wills was the greatest sin he could commit against them. Why did he plead with them so? Why did he not insist upon their following him? Was he so weak willed as to leave his dear wife and little babes in the hands of destruction while he pursued relief from his own burden? What of their burdens? Were they not his as well? Even after being pressed about it by an acquaintance named Charity, the matter of his wife and children is left to the powers of persuasion rather than election. Here is how the conversation went:

"Then said Charity to Christian, Have you a family? Are you a married man?

Chr. I have a Wife and four small Children.

Char. And why did you not bring them along with you?

Chr. Then Christian wept, and said, Oh how willingly would I have done it, but they were all of them utterly averse to my going on Pilgrimage.

Char. But you should have talked to them, and have endeavoured to have shewn them the danger of being behind.

Chr. So I did, and told them also what God had shewed to me of the destruction of our City; but I seemed to them as one that mocked, and they believed me not.

Char. And did you pray to God that he would bless your counsel to them?

Chr. Yes, and that with much affection; for you must think that my Wife and poor Children were very dear unto me.

Char. But did you tell them of your own sorrow, and fear of destruction? For I suppose that destruction was visible enough to you.

Chr. Yes, over, and over, and over. They might also see my fears in my countenance, in my tears, and also in my trembling under the apprehension of the Judgment that did hang over our heads; but all was not sufficient to prevail with them to come with me.

Char. But what could they say for themselves, why they came not?

Chr. Why, my Wife was afraid of losing this World, and my Children were given to the foolish Delights of youth: so what by one thing, and what by another, they left me to wander in this manner alone.

Char. But did you not with your vain life, damp all that you by words used by way of persuasion to bring them away with you?

Chr. Indeed I cannot commend my life; for I am conscious to myself of many failings therein: I know also, that a man by his conversation may soon overthrow, what by argument or persuasion he doth labour to fasten upon others for their good. Yet, this I can say, I was very wary of giving them occasion, by any unseemly action, to make them averse to going on Pilgrimage. Yea, for this very thing they would tell me I was too precise, and that I denied myself of things (for their sakes) in which they saw no evil. Nay, I think I may say, that if what they saw in me did hinder them, it was in my great tenderness in sinning against God, or of doing any wrong to my Neighbor.

Char. Indeed Cain hated his Brother, because his own works were evil, and his Brother's righteous; and if thy Wife and Children have been offended with thee for this, they thereby shew themselves to be implacable to good, and thou hast delivered thy soul from their blood."

Oh, poor Christian! Your wife abhors you and your children will not heed you! Oh, poor Christian! Oh, how you pleaded with them! Oh, how you suffered under their rejection. If you only could have pleaded the more! If you only had the right words to say! Then maybe your wife would have followed you! Then maybe your little children would have become convinced! Oh, poor man! You did all you could, did you not?

But what if Charity had been wiser? Would he have been less charitable? What if he had told Christian the truth? Maybe the conversation would have transpired a little bit more like this:

Then said Charity to Christian, Have you a family? Are you a married man?

Chr. I have a Wife and four small Children.

Char. And why did you not bring them along with you?

Chr. Then Christian wept, and said, Oh how willingly would I have done it, but they were all of them utterly averse to my going on Pilgrimage.

Char. But are they not baptized? Are they not as much children of God as yourself?

Chr. Even so, they would not come. My wife is prone to obstinance at times and much affection for the world, and my children are not yet of age for baptism, for they are still yet immature in spiritual matters. But I pleaded with them fervently and told them also what God had shewed to me of the destruction of our City; but I seemed to them as one that mocked, and they believed me not.

Char. But why would a wife mock her husband? Why would small children ridicule their father? Have you no honor in their eyes? Have they no respect for your discernment? Are you not the head over them as Christ is your head? Even Noah, the only righteous man upon the earth, would not venture such a journey upon the seas without his wife and sons. Even Lot was shewn mercy in the city of destruction as the Lord brought his wife and daughters to safety, taking them by the hand, intoxicated as they were by the world.

Chr. But I pleaded with them over, and over, and over. They might also see my fears in my countenance, in my tears, and also in my trembling under the apprehension of the Judgment that did hang over our heads; but all was not sufficient to prevail with them to come with me.

Char. Did you reason with them, then?

Chr. Oh, I did sir. Reason I did, until I became vile in their sight. But my wife was afraid of losing this world, and my children were given to the foolish delights of youth: so what by one thing, and what by another, they left me to wander in this manner alone.

Char. And did you pray to God that he would bless your counsel to them?

Chr. Yes, and that with much affection; for you must think that my wife and poor children were very dear unto me.

Char. Why, then, did you reason with them so, for did you not know that as many as received Him, to them He gave the right to become children of God, to those who believe in His name: who were born not of blood, nor of the will of the flesh, nor of the will of man, but of God? Why did you not take your wife by the hand and lead her upon this journey together? Why did you not lift your little children unto your breast and carry them upon your back in order to lead them away from the impending destruction? Are your prayers without action? Are you so inclined to embark upon the difficulties of divine prayer only to leave it for the ease of human persuasion?

Chr. Indeed I cannot commend my life; for I am conscious to myself of many failings therein.

Char. Go back, then. Return to the city of destruction. Risk your soul for the sake of those entrusted to your care. Ensure that your children have been washed by the waters of baptism. See to it that your wife knows that you are willing to give your own life for the sake of hers. Commend them to God, not with words of human reason, but with words of divine promise. Go to them and snatch them straight away from that damnable city. For they too belong to Christ. Let them not suffer, then, under the dominion of Satan.

What if it happened this way? The story would be quite different indeed. There would have been no need for a part II, where Christian's wife, Christiana, takes her children and embarks upon the same journey her husband undertook so many years before. Yes, it is true. Christiana did make the journey as well, for she made it upon her own volition. And what are we to learn from The Pilgrim's Progress if not that the Christian journey is an endeavor of the human will – that it is a purely inward and individual journey. Yes, we learn something truly contrary to Biblical revelation. We learn that salvation is an experience quite unlike an ecclesiastical life, quite unlike a life of a present kingdom influence. It is a life where baptism is either unnecessary or insignificant and the souls of our posterity are completely out of our hands. It is a life which has come to dominate the theology of our own age, in Baptist churches certainly, but not only in Baptist churches. The importance of baptism and the covenantal nurture of children has been minimized even amongst the sacramental crowd. We must ask ourselves: Is this really the progress which we pilgrims seek?

22

A MULTI-GENERATIONAL VISION

"To Him be glory in the church by Christ Jesus to all generations, forever and ever. Amen." (Eph. 3:21)

When it comes to eschatology, the study of the kingdom of Christ as it moves from the present to the future, there are a few different perspectives Christians tend to embrace. One group asks: "Why bother to polish the brass on a sinking ship?" – implying that as the ship goes down, it is the souls on board that are the only things worth saving. Another group insists: "By all means, polish the brass on a sinking ship" – implying that there is more to our duty than the saving of souls. A third group insists: "The ship is not sinking!" – all the while their heads bobbing up and down about the waves.

The ship is the world. Is it sinking or not? Is the world in which we live spiraling downward, or is it being built up and strengthened? I suppose the answer is both, really. I suppose the answer depends on what you choose to see. Do you choose to see the depravity? Do you choose to see the increasing sinfulness in your immediate environment? Are you comparing your world to what it was like one hundred years ago, forgetting what it was like one thousand years ago? If so, your perspective might cause you to become a pessimist. You see only the crumbling of mountains, never bothering to watch where the avalanche falls. You fail to see that all destruction creates a new foundation, that a myriad of ancient cities lie beneath the streets of new ones. Like that great pessimist of old, Chicken Little, you keep waiting for the sky to fall. And maybe one day it will. And when it does, you will say, "I told you so." But if it does, will your heart sink at the sight of an even brighter sky that was hiding behind the first all the while?

It is easy to become the pessimist. It is easy to look at a culture and get caught up in the immediate consequences. It is more difficult to look ahead. Or even to look behind. Looking ahead takes vision. Looking behind takes work. But the past will always give you a glimpse into the future. The future will always remind us of something in the past. The reason is that the same God is the ruler of both. The same Christ is the Christ of the past, present, and future. The same church was in the beginning and evermore will be. There is an immutability to our changing environment. It will only change as far as the Author is willing for it to change, and it will never change beyond the scope of his artistry. There is a plan in place. There is a story that has already been written. It is presently being played out upon the stage. Its author and audience are one and the same.

When God told Abram to look up into the sky and count the stars, he knew they were beyond Abram's ability to count, not because Abram was a poor mathematician, but because there were so many stars. "So shall your offspring be," (Gen. 15:5) God said. God is the only one who is able to sort the beginning from the end. God is the only one who sees both beginning and end at the same time. As the mountain crumbles, God sees precisely where it will land, for he has determined where it will land, and he has determined the reason for its landing. He has already determined which cities will be laid to waste and which cities will be built anew. "Whatever the Lord pleases He does, in heaven and in earth." (Ps. 135:6) Do not think for a minute that Abram should have been able to count the stars. Do not think for a minute that if you were Abram, that you would have been able to count them, for "The earth is the Lord's, and all its fullness, the world and all those who dwell therein." (Ps. 24:1)

God is bigger than the stars. At this point you might accuse me of stating the obvious, and so be it. But if it is so obvious that

God is bigger than the stars, then why do we have such a hard time understanding that he is bigger than our children? Yes, that is what this inevitably comes down to – that even our children, our very offspring, belong to God. "The earth is the Lord's, and all its fullness…" Why is it, then, so difficult for the church to come to grips and have unity in the fact that our children are God's children and that baptism is God's mark upon them? "Your kingdom is an everlasting kingdom, and Your dominion endures throughout all generations." (Ps. 145:13)

Paul acknowledges this in his letter to the Ephesians. He mentions that it is for Christ's glory that the church consists of multiple generations. There is no favoritism in the affections of God. He is God to both rich and poor. He is God to both male and female. He is God to both Jew and Gentile. And yes, he is God to both young and old. He is the Lord over all generations. And this is his church. Remember, there is but one body and one Spirit. There is but one Lord, one faith, and one baptism. There is "one God and Father of all, who is above all and through all, and in you all." (Eph. 4:5-6) There is no mystery kept hidden here. Children are as much a part of the church as any one of us. Children are as much part of Christ's kingdom as the next. The body of Christ is made up of all sorts of people, children included. God is a God whose "faithfulness endures to all generations." (Ps. 119:90)

As Christians, as the body of Christ, it is imperative that we look forward. It is crucial that we have a vision bigger than ourselves. It is critical that, though we are unable to count the stars, we recognize that God has already counted them. If the ship is sailing aright, we must understand that it might at any time go asunder. If the ship is sinking we must recognize that there will be other ships coming behind. If the mountain crumbles, we must know that sometimes things must be broken before they can be restored. It is important as people of God that we have a multi-generational vision for our families and for our children as Christ's kingdom moves forward. We must go on polishing the brass no matter whether the ship is sinking or not, for that is compatible with the character of our God. Our God gives up on nothing and no one, not even the smallest, not even the weakest, especially not the humblest, among us. If he has determined it, it will come to pass. It he has claimed it for his own, it will not fall. This is what we must never forget moving forward. This is what we must embrace as we seek unity within the body of Christ. This is what we must remember when we consider what is to become of our children.

But there is an irony about. A multi-generational vision is not unique to the sacramentalists. There are many who share this productive vision for the future, this vision for their children, who will not allow them the waters of baptism. They believe wholeheartedly that their children belong to the Lord; they teach them vigorously the Word of God; they pray for them; they multiply them; they joyfully anticipate what their family tree might look like one hundred years from now. They understand the importance of children, but they devalue the importance of baptism. For them, I hope this book has been helpful in shedding some light upon the latter while re-enforcing the former. I hope they might learn to fully give their children over to the Lord.

Then there are their opposites. There are those who baptize their children. They are quite familiar with the covenantal rhetoric. They understand the continuity between the testaments. Abraham is their hero. They sincerely thank God every time a little baby is sprinkled over the head with water, and they giggle incessantly every time the sleeping babe's peaceful countenance turns sour and every time she begins to cry at the surprise deluge streaming down her little cheeks. They get it. They understand. But, somehow, so often it seems, they don't *really* get it. They don't fully understand the significance of what that baby baptism means. Like Christian in The Pilgrim's Progress, they don't claim their children for Christ.

They still treat them as if they needed conversion. They don't want to have too many of them, for it would only make things more difficult, and who knows if they are even elect anyhow? They could care less what happens one hundred years down the road, for tomorrow will take care of itself. Everything they do is for today. There is no multi-generational vision to be had. For them, I hope they begin to see that baptism is not only a form of religion, but that it contains the very promises of God. I hope they understand not only that baptism is important, but that it is useful, that belonging to God has generational implications. I hope they notice, when they look up into the sky, that God is bigger than the stars. And for all of us, when we examine the ship, I hope we notice that whether it sinks or whether it sails, that there is an awful lot of brass that still needs polishing.

23

CONCLUDING PRACTICAL INQUIRIES

To be clear, baptism is not the entire gospel. We must not go around preaching baptism as if it was Christ himself. But to be equally clear, baptism *is* gospel. The gospel is incomplete without it. Compare this to the Word of God. The words on the page are not the gospel. The Scriptures carry the gospel. They are a means to the gospel. However, the magic of the Scriptures is that Christ himself is the Word of God. He is the eternal Logos. So as Christ is recognized in the Scriptures, as the Scriptures become not only words on a page but a living Spirit, as Christ is proclaimed and revealed, the Scriptures can be said to be gospel. Christ alone is the gospel. The Scriptures are the revelation of Christ. They are an immediate portal to him, and as a portal, it can be said that the Scriptures are the gospel. But this is also true with baptism. That is why baptism may be called the Word made visible. Baptism may be more limited than the Scriptures as to the scope and depth of its interaction with mankind, but it is no less powerful or efficacious. Baptism does the same thing the Scriptures do. They both lead us to Christ. They both reveal Christ. They both carry the gospel to us as well as carry us to the gospel. They are both necessary in so far as Christ is to be most fully encountered.

Word and sacraments. These are the focal point of the Reformation. These are the formal means of grace. In these is the revelation of Jesus Christ, and around these does the church operate. Baptism is a sacrament. It was practiced by Christ, instituted by Christ, and commanded by Christ. Baptism is a ritual. It is a religious ceremonial cleansing. It was practiced under the Old Testament as a priestly ritual and made common by Christ under the New Testament. It replaced circumcision as the sign of the gospel. Christ made it the rite of initiation into his church. Yes, Christ came to establish a church. A society. A government upon his shoulders. That was his mission. He came to gather followers and justify the world to himself through sacrifice. He came to establish righteousness upon the earth. He called this the kingdom of Heaven. His church is the manifestation of that kingdom. He came to bring people from darkness to light, from death to life. He made them part of his body. He called it his church. He created it out of Jews and Gentiles, males and females, adults and their children. Yes, their children. Jesus always accepted the children. Never did he turn them away.

Word and sacraments. These are focal points of redemption. These are the formal means of grace. In these is the revelation of Jesus Christ, and around these does the church operate. Baptism is a sacrament. Baptism is initiation into the body of Christ. It is a right for the children of God, not because they are worthy, but because God is worthy. Children have a right to baptism. To deny them baptism is to deny them Christ. Who would ever want to attempt that?

Who would ever want to hold back the children from coming to the Lord? Is that not what baptism is? Coming to the Lord? Who would drive wedges within the Christian household? Is there such a thing as a Christian household? Or are there only Christian individuals? What relationship do our children have with God? Are they not special in his sight? Or is there no distinction between Christian children and the children of Baal? Must we wait upon the Lord to change the hearts of our children before they are baptized? What if he never does? What if there was something we could have done? What if our passivity becomes our folly? What if we could have brought them before the Lord in baptism? Why is it that so many Christian children, when disciplined in Christian graces, grow up to remain Christians?

Why is it that so many unbelieving households raise children to become unbelievers? Where is God in all this? Where is election in all this? Should we not expect God to save his elect from out of the world just as much as from believing households? Then why do most believers come from believing homes? What are we teaching our children when we deny them baptism? Are we teaching them that God's grace is dependent upon their own merit? Or volition? Or conformity? Are we teaching them that the Lord is not their God until they grow a little bit older, and a little bit older, and a little bit older? Why is he not their God when they are but babes? Or is God's favor dependent upon their cognitive abilities? Should we wait until they understand before they are baptized? Understand what exactly? That God is merciful? Cannot even the smallest child rest in God's mercy? Does not even the lowest babe know his offenses? If not in words, then perhaps in thought? Yes, how do we know the thoughts of the child? How do we dare keep the child from the means of grace just because we fail to discern his thoughts? Or are we unbelievers ourselves? Do we disbelieve that the Holy Spirit would really work through something so menial as common water? Do we expect something more from the Spirit? Something greater? Something more extraordinary? Why do we wait in vain when the grace is set before our children in the waters of baptism? What do our children learn? Are they not ever watchful? Are they not ever mindful? Do they not learn to doubt when we tell them that they are not ready? Do they not grow insecure when we encourage them to be cautious with God? What if they love him? Do we squelch that love? What if they desire him? Do we hinder that desire? And what if they don't love him? Do we tell them that they are not his? Yes, what if they don't love him? Do we accept they are children of Hell? Do we not tell them that they are God's children and that God loves them and requires – no, not only requires – but longs for their love in return? Do we not treat them as Christians? Do we not treat them as fellow members of the body of Christ? Do we not treat them as heirs of the kingdom? Or do we treat them like the dogs that they are?

If you are a Christian – a member of the body of Christ – if you are a believer, you did not become a believer on your own accord. It was not due to your impeccable intellect. It was not because of your innate wisdom or strong will. It was not on account of your sincerity. Nor was it due to any goodness in you. It was because of God's mercy. God looked upon you, even before you were born, and set his love upon you. He decreed it. In his power, he brought it to pass. God drew you to himself. He called you, and he made sure that you answered. This is called grace. Why would it be any different for our children?

If you are a Christian – a member of the body of Christ – if you have children, then God has laid claim to them. The promise that has been given to you, the promise of the Holy Spirit upon which you rest your hope, this promise has been given to your children as well. Can you not see how applicable baptism is? Baptism is not only a matter for theology books. It is a matter of parenting. Deciding what to do with your children in regards to the waters of baptism, in regards to membership in the church, is a matter of raising your children. Do we wait upon God and hope for the best? Or do we lead them beside the still waters so that they may drink? Do we treat them as bastard children? As half-breeds? Or do we treat them as Christians? As joint heirs with Christ? Do we teach them to doubt God's Word or to believe and embrace it? Are these not questions of parenting? Are these matters of parenting not of supreme importance as the kingdom of Heaven moves forth and grows upon this earth?

There are two needs at stake. One, of course, is that children of believers need to be baptized into Christ, into membership in his church. But it should be clear that baptism is not enough. There are plenty of dead bones in the waters of baptism, bones that were left there by presumptuous parents and neglectful ministers. Yes, there is a great stench that rises up out of the waters of baptism, permeating the sanctuary, the homes and the streets, even rising to the very nostrils of God himself, and he no doubt turns his face from the rotten odor. Just because one is baptized does not mean that one will be saved. No one will ever be saved apart from perseverance in faith.

But just because the road is difficult does not mean it should be avoided. The road that begins with baptism is the road that leads to salvation, but it must be travelled upon. And simply because there are some who misuse it does not mean that it should be neglected. Just because there are some who are baptized who decide the road is too difficult to continue does not mean that we should devalue baptism. No, on the contrary. It means that we must be more diligent with the second need – the need to walk in newness of life. Just because the road is difficult does not mean, in regards to our children, that we should wait upon God for another road to open up. There is no other road! The road that starts at baptism is the road of Christ. We must bring our children with us no matter how difficult. We must not wait upon our children. If so, consider what we are teaching them. Are we not teaching them, then, to doubt that God's promises are multi-generational? Are we not teaching them, then, that God cares less for children as he does for adults, or that the way to Christ comes by another means other than divine grace?

AMEN

ENDNOTES

Chapter 1
1. Laws and customs were integral to the Jewish religious system. Though this point is inferred, it would make sense that the teachers of the law were discussing the law.
2. Leviticus 16:4 describes the sacrifice of atonement. Exodus 29:1-4 describes the preparation for priesthood

Chapter 2
1. Catechism of the Catholic Church, part 2, article 2, section 1, no. 1116
2. Westminster Shorter Catechism (WSC) no. 92
3. Westminster Confession of Faith (WCF) 1646 Ch. 27, article 2
4. The Book of Common Prayer (BOCP) composed 1563-1571, catechism, the sacraments, 1st question

Chapter 3
1. The Augsburg Confession (AC) article 9.1 & .2
2. 2nd Helvetic Confession composed 1562-1564 ch.20 under What it Means...
3. BOCP, Thirty Nine Articles of Religion, article 27, The Church Hymnal Corporation and Seabury Press, certified 1979
4. WCF ch28, article 1
5. The Confession of Faith of the Evangelical United Brethren Church, article 6. In 1968 the EUBC merged with the Methodist Church taking the name United Methodist and incorporating the confessional statement of the EUBC
6. Luther's Small Catechism (LSC) section 4; question first, second, and third; taken from the Book of Concord readers edition 2005, Concordia Publishing House
7. The Belgic Confession, article 34

Chapter 4
1. The London Baptist Confession of Faith (LBCF) also called the 2nd London Confession, Ch. 28, article 1; Ch. 29, articles 1 & 2

Chapter 6
1. From Rock of Ages, Augustus Toplady 1740-1778

Chapter 7
1. 1 Corinthians 16:13; 2 Corinthians 13:15; Colossians 1:23 – just to name a few examples
2. The Polemics of Infant Baptism, B.B. Warfield, 1899

Chapter 8

1. Clovis was king of the Franks in the 5th Century. He was successful in consolidating the tribes under one rule, and his conversion was effective in Christianizing the region of Gaul.
2. LSC, the sacrament of holy baptism, third part

Chapter 11

1. WCF Ch. 25, article 2

Chapter 12

1. WCF, Ch. 27, article 2
2. LSC Explanation, The Sacraments, question 236
3. LSC Explanation, The Sacraments, section 2, The Blessings of Baptism

Chapter 13

1. BOCP, the catechism, holy baptism, 3rd question
2. WCF, Ch. 28, article 1
3. Westminster Larger Catechism, question 165
4. LSC Explanation, question 254

Chapter 14

1. Peter, Susan, Edmund, & Lucy from The Lion, the Witch, and the Wardrobe by C.S. Lewis. While playing Hide-and-Seek, Lucy enters a wardrobe which leads her into Narnia.

Chapter 15

1. BOCP, 39 Articles of Religion, article, 25
2. WCF, Ch. 25, article 2

Chapter 17

1. John 4:46-54, Mark 7:24-30, & Mark 9:14-29 are a few examples

Chapter 18

1. Acts 16:15, Acts 16:33, 1 Corinthians 1:16 – though not proving there were infants in the households, these passages show continuity with the Old Testament paradigm.

Chapter 19

1. Systematic Theology, Charles Hodge, part 3, Ch. 20, sections 10,11

Final apologia

When I mention that the practice of baptizing children is a matter of the gospel, I am not saying that it is impossible to be saved without it. I am arguing, rather, that it is a matter of ecclesiastical purity. When I call the Baptists dissenters, I am not saying they have abandoned Christ or the church, but only that they have abandoned the commonality of confession and embrace teachings which have obscured the gospel and the church, and this obscuring has caused dissention in the applications of the Christ. I believe that the primary problem with baptistic theology is that it tends to divorce the gospel message from the ekklesia and the eschaton. It results in an isolated understanding of soteriology – a salvation separate from the church and the coming kingdom. It is my intention to maintain peace within the brotherhood of believers, and I do not wish to disparage any, but I am convinced that the consequences of baptistic theology are at the very least a problem for gospel unity and that it is not only a problem for Baptists, but it is also a problem for paedobaptists who have adopted a baptistic theology of children. It is my hope that one day the practice of including children in the ordinance of baptism into the Body of Christ will once again become widespread, and not only so, but that we would recapture the vision of nurturing our children accordingly.

About the Author

Chase McMaster is the founder of Pilgrim Voyage Press, a publishing company dedicated to promoting truth, beauty, and goodness in literature. He is mostly a Presbyterian, formerly a Baptist, and currently an Anglican. He is a graduate of The Master's College.

Acknowledgements

Thank you to those who have provided your criticisms, suggestions, and direction:

Rev. Virgil Hurt
Rev. Steve Walker
Dr. Phil Olsson
Rev. James Knapton
Rev. Edward Dondi
My remarkable wife, Jennifer